INDIE INSIDER

FUNDAMENTALS

EPISODE ONE

CHELSEA CAMARON
RYAN MICHELE

Published: May 10, 2017

Editing by: C & D Editing

Cover Design: Susan Garwood at Wicked Women Designs

This work is intended for mature audiences only. Please do not buy if explicit language offends you.

This is not meant to be an exact depiction of life as an author, but rather a work meant to bring on a laugh or two and help someone else. These are our experiences and opinions.

Blurb

Have you ever thought about life behind the pages? Have you ever wondered what an author goes through? Have you considered writing a book but don't know what to do with it?

Well, the *Indie Insider* is here for you.

No, this is not a how-to guide. This is a real, raw, uncut, behind the scenes sight from two established authors. What works for one person may not work for another, but there will be something you can take away from this.

Even if you are just curious, this is a book that will entertain as well as encourage. If you're already established, happy in your writing life, this book will only offer you the solace that the times you have been down you were not alone. If you are just starting out, struggling, or just at a standstill, then this book is here to motivate and educate.

Sit back, grab a drink, and take a look inside the mind of an Indie author today.

Please note, this is Indie Insider: *Fundamentals. As the first episode in this serial, you will find this to be an overview that briefly touches on a multitude of subjects an Indie author faces. If the series is well received, there will be additional volumes to come where we will breakdown the items here and so much more in detail.*

TABLE OF CONTENTS

Introductions are in order

Ryan

You're probably thinking, who are these two chicks and why should I read what they have to say. You totally don't have to as this is just our opinions, but let me tell you a little about me. I'm Ryan Michele and live in a small town in central Illinois, with my two girls and husband. My favorite place to be is on my huge bed-swing my husband made me that looks over our pond.

I've been in the Indie world writing for four years. I was a teacher before turning to writing full time, which was a difficult decision to make. So far, I have twenty-five books under my belt. This one makes twenty-six. The genre's I write in span the spectrum. All the way from MC Romance to Paranormal Romance to New Adult Romance to Mafia Romance. Throw in a bit of Erotic Romance and sprinkle it in with some Billionaires and there you have me.

I've been through the ups and downs that is the Indie world over the last few years and have picked up some things that could help you. I'm all for sharing what I know with my thoughts. I've made tons of mistakes. Tons. Many I would take back and change in a heartbeat. Unfortunately, I can't do that. Instead I have to learn from those mistakes and move on.

Indie Insider is my way of answering many questions I get from other authors in a way that is fun and relatable (I hope). Thank you so much for taking the time to read our thoughts. We don't know everything, but hope that you come away with learning at least one thing from this book. If that happens, then we've done our job.

Enjoy! ~Ryan

Chelsea

Hello out there! I'm Chelsea Camaron and well, I write books. Whew, that introduction stuff is always awkward for me. I'm a small town girl from the Crystal Coast of North Carolina. I live on a farm with my hubbub (husband), two kiddos, and my dog – Sheba and yes she is the Queen. I love lazy Carolina days and can be found working on my front porch most of the time.

I have been self-publishing for four years and in 2015, I signed my first traditional publishing contract with Penguin Random House. I am what is considered a hybrid author. At this time, I have 40 releases behind me and so many more to come. I am a USA Today bestselling author, if that is important to you – though in the course of Indie Insider, I hope you will learn a title is great, but it doesn't define you or me. I write contemporary romance, romantic suspense, and psychological thrillers.

In my time in this book world, I have made more mistakes than I can count. Over the years, I have learned, I have failed, and I have seen some success. Most importantly, I've made partnerships, friendships, and it has taught me even more.

Indie Insider was born with a late night text to Ryan Michele. This is a way for us to share our experiences both good and bad. Yes, I said it, we share the bad too. Our hope is that we can be an encouragement to all – no matter where you are in your writing career. We don't have all the answers and what may work for us may not work for you, but if we don't ever try how can we know?

You will find there are sections where Ryan Michele and I do things much the same, then you will also see where we are oh so very different. We hope by taking these differences and combining them we will be able to help you from most angles.

Writing is a personal thing. Publishing is a personal thing. The decisions you will be asked to make are again personal. We have set up Indie Insider to be about your mindset. Each section will have questions for you to ask yourself.

In all my time in this book world, the one thing that has pushed me through is my mindset. We hope that we are able to help you get the mindset that is one for long term success. And your success – well, it's defined by you because everyone views success differently.

Thank you and stay encouraged!

Connect with us

Have a question, comment or concern? Please email us at indieinsiderbook@gmail.com

Want more Indie Insider? Join our:
   FB Page

Want even more?? Join our:
   FB Group

We love to hear from you!
   Chelsea & Ryan

Dear Reader

Dear reader, author, aspiring author, blogger, or curious person (yup you),

Welcome to the *Indie Insider*!

Books. Books. Books. That's why you found us. Either you're already an Indie Author or you're aspiring to be one. Or, well hell, you're just here to see what us two crazy chicks have gotten ourselves into this time. Either way, Welcome!

If you think this is a how-to book, hold up a minute. Nope, this is a book by two authors who have been writing in the Indie world for four years. This is a book from our perspective, which is not the perspective of everyone in this industry by a long shot. It is not a guide for you to live by and worship.

What it is are things we learned over the years. Things we came across that stand out to us. Some that work for us, and some that went to shit quickly. Now, be smart and be you. Something that works for us, may not work for you. Hell, things that work for Chelsea don't work for me. And vice versa.

Please be advised: the language in this book will contain cussing. We write bikers; it happens. If you can't handle it, stop now, because we don't wish to offend. This book is a real take from two very real Indie authors and what we have seen and felt. It is not the opinions of others, and if you don't agree, please don't think it came from anyone but us.

The Indie world has blown up over the past few years. Where there was once no way for us authors to publish without going through an agent and formal publisher is no more. Now, books pop up so rapidly on the Zon (that's Amazon) that we get whiplash half the time. This is great, but it's also mudding down your visibility. It's a fact, so suck it up and deal.

The more books, the more our readers have to choose from. This is a good thing. Why? Because how many books do you plan on putting out a year? A reader (me) can read a book in a day or two and be ready for more blood. Can you put out a book every day or two? No, it's not physically possible. This is why readers having a wide variety is great.

This is also a double-edged sword, because you don't want your readers to forget about you. This is why building relationships with your readers is so important. Hopefully, you'll learn some techniques for this in our book.

You'll see this book is set up into sections. You'll have *Chelsea's Chats* and *Ryan's Ramblings*. Each one of these are from our own perspectives. We don't do everything the same. We don't have all the same things in place. But, if one of our own experiences works for you, then you taking the time to read this is a serious score in my book.

You'll also see names pop up. These can range from editors, proofreaders, cover designers, photogs, formatters, other authors we've learned from, or really about anything. It's all in an attempt to open your horizons and see there are many options out there for you.

If you think you're going to read this and become a billionaire … just stop reading right now. If my ass was a billionaire, I'd be on a damn beach somewhere sipping a drink with a kindle in my hand and not in cold-ass Illinois. *And I, Chelsea, would make sure she took my ass with her because* hello, *beach is my favorite word, like, ever. It's up there with fuck.*

We hope that you find some of these things helpful. We'd also love to hear from you. If there is something in this book you'd like to see more about, or if you have a topic you'd like us to cover that we haven't, please email us at indieinsiderbook@gmail.com and drop us a line. Now, if you're going to cuss us out, that email doesn't work. It's bogus and a figment of your imagination. This is the sarcasm you will see in this book. Take it with a grain of salt. And yes, the email does work and we'd love to hear from you. Even the curses, but be prepared, I like to curse back. *Ha!*

Also, this book is written more conversationally. As in, you're sitting in front of me and we're having a talk. I, Ryan, don't use grammatically correct words, because I don't speak them. You're gonna see the word "gonna"! Like how I tossed that in there. Also, from me, you'll see a lot of contractions and I use the word alright instead of all right. It's me.

You'll notice Chelsea has more of a technical way to her words, but that's all her. She's a master at it. You want to write technically perfect, she's your chick to watch. Definitely not me! Like, see, I, Chelsea, would say: you will notice Chelsea has a more technical writing style. There are places for contractions and places they don't actually belong and every word has a purpose, place, and fundamental way it should be used. Now, in the Indie world, this is both a blessing and a curse because, you, my dear friend, can get by with a lot more grammatical and slang slides that are technically wrong, but it's your world so you can do it. You just need to understand that, if your goal is to be traditionally published, well, there is a different style of writing they are looking for.

Writing styles, editing styles, these are things that Ryan and I have spent a lot of time conversing about over the years. This book may not cover it all. We aren't trying to leave something out. We just don't think about every single thing in this edition. You want to know something specific, see the email address above and reach out.

Look, no intimidation, all joking aside, we're not celebrities. We are people. Anyone who has ever said the word fangirl to me, Chelsea, knows

I will say nothing to fangirl here, but you're welcome to be my friend. I'm a small-town girl with an imagination. I am sugary sweet unless I'm angry, so please do not be afraid to ask anything. We want to help.

This will not encompass every publishing step. It's not that kind of thing. If this is well-received, maybe in the future we will walk you through the process on a project with us. Who knows? This is just our way to give a little to those who care to see it.

Sit back, grab a Diet Coke or coffee thingy that I can't pronounce, and let's get on with the show! That totally sounded like we're in a circus. But I guess, in a way, we are.

Chelsea & Ryan

18

CHAPTER ONE

CONCEPT: LIGHT BULB ... AND THE IDEA COMES!

S o, you have an idea! Magic, unicorns, glitter, rainbows, and champagne. It's a celebration.

STOP right there!

ASK YOURSELF THESE QUESTIONS:
1. Is this idea original?
2. Is this something I can see myself reading over and over again?
3. Do I expect to make money?

Chelsea's Chat:

YES, we said it: STOP. Now, look, I'll be frank, I'm a dream chaser. I believe every single person should be able to go after their dreams. Hold nothing back and really go for it.

So, why am I telling you to stop? Well, because this is a business, and therefore, you need to have your business mindset in place going in. The biggest mistake I ever made in my career was simply going in. My very first book was a joke, literally. It was a bucket list thing to do. This is a business, not a thing to do. If there is one thing that will carry you through the ups and downs of this book world—the self-publishing industry— it's your mindset. If you write like it's something to do, fine; but know that your future will reflect your mindset. If you write like you plan to make millions, well, you are going to be signing up for some therapy quick, because the money isn't what you expect.

Get your mind right and the rest will follow. Legit, real deal, my career has lasted and continues because of my mindset.

I do not care what anyone else does, as long as they don't plagiarize because, people, that is WRONG! Be original. You are beautiful just the way you are. Show you, own you, love you, and don't be someone else.

So, you got your mind right, great. The idea is there. But ask yourself, really ask now: did this come from a movie, another book, television? What inspired the concept? If your idea is based *entirely* off someone else's concept, there is a world for that.

Hold on tight. I said it. There is a world for using someone else's shit. You ready for it? Fan fiction.

It's real.

In fan fiction, it's acceptable to use someone else's "world." Fan fiction is a public domain, and therefore, cannot be sold. Yes, I said that shit, too. You cannot make money on someone else's concept unless you have a contract to do so (example: Kindle Worlds, ghost writing, biographies).

I want to be clear that sometimes we find inspiration in other works, but please make the concept your own. Being inspired to make something your way is not fan fiction, but copying someone's shit and making name changes or the likes, well, that's wrong, okay? Some of the most popular romance books to date were inspired by something else, but the world was created to stand on its own.

If you even have to question if this is similar to someone else's work, then back off. While plagiarism is categorized as copying someone word for word and an idea technically can't be copyrighted nor can a name, you need to make sure your brand isn't known for ripping off other people.

Don't be the Indie author who gives all Indie's a bad name. There, I said it. If you don't want someone to copy your concept … well, folks, don't do it to someone else. *Duh*.

Now, inspiration comes from different places, so as long as your concept is unique, then yes, you will find inspiration from other places and people. But make it your own.

Okay, so your idea is your own. What's next? Well, is this an idea you can read over and over and over and over and over and over again? Too many overs? Nope. In fact, if you don't think you can read your concept and story at least five times, then you need not go there.

This is a marathon, not a sprint.

By the time I finish a book, I feel like I know my hero and heroine better than I know myself. Sometimes, **gasp** I even don't love them as much as I did because I have had too much time with them. Yes, I am giving you the truth. My own characters get on my nerves sometimes. But you know what, if I don't believe in the concept, I can't get through the many read throughs it takes to finish my projects. Then I walk away because: why punish myself?

You have to believe in yourself before anyone else can believe in you!

Okay, so you have an original idea, and you know you can read it every day for the rest of the year and still be in love with it. Now, you just know you have the next bestseller. You are spending the money before you even type the first word in your mind because you know you're going to make cake (that's our term for lots of money).

WRONG!

Let me tell you from experience, just because a book makes a bestseller list, does not mean it made money. Yes, I said it. Some books list, but they don't actually profit right away.

Truth: It costs thousands to release a novel. Yes, thousands.

Truth: Pricing is everything. If you sell your book for $0.99, then you will make only $0.35 a copy sold (let's not get into returns right now). You invested $3K into your book and want to debut strong so you give it a $0.99 price point. It takes 8,572 units before you make a profit.

By the way, most sites pay authors 60 days after the close of the month. So, while you are trying to sell 10K copies so you can be profitable, you also have to pay your bills and have the money to cover your next release while you wait two months to see the first penny back on your original $3K investment.

Scary? Hell yes! I'm not putting this out there to scare you, but to keep shit real. *One Ride* (*Hellions Ride* Book 1) is probably by far my best seller to date as units move. Guess what? It never made a real bestseller list. Yup, I said "real list" (yes, it made the Amazon overall top 100 more than 5 times, Barnes and Noble top 100, iBooks top 100 more than twice), but nope, my beloved *Hellions* series never made *USA Today*, *Wall Street*

Journal, or *NYT* (we will get into lists much later, so hang tight. That reality is coming for you, too, and you will be surprised).

That book alone cost me $5K in its original release. No joke! It released December 20, 2013, and yes, in eleven days, I made back my investment, but that was it. Yes, release month only covered my expenses, so I didn't actually see a profit in my checking account until March 30, 2014 when I got paid for January 2014 sales. My *Love and Repair* series, six books and my first series to this day, has not made back the money I invested in the series. Yes, six books, and I still haven't made a profit on any of them! I wrote them because I have a passion to write, to tell a story. I fucked them up, and I'm still learning and fixing. *Stay*, a book that is meant to be a mind fuck, I wrote for myself and guess what? It took me a solid fourteen months and three blog tours before I finally made a profit on that particular title.

Now, if you ask readers which of my books they absolutely loved and stuck with them, the majority will tell you *Stay*. It wasn't mainstream, and it didn't catch (these are things we will go into more detail with later, but yes, being mainstream matters if you want money. Yet, it's a challenge all its own). I still love *Stay*, I'm still proud of it, but it has taken me a lot to see a profit, and I have to be thankful for the other books that make enough to carry the weight of the books that don't sell enough.

If you are planning to be an author because of the money, rethink your strategy. Yes, money can be made, but your mindset must be on your business. It's not going to roll in overnight.

No, this is not meant to discourage. I make a living, a very comfortable one. However, I'm not a millionaire and nowhere near it. Okay? Got me?

Yes, some people have seen success on a debut, but it's rare. And making a bestselling list once doesn't promise every release you have will make a list.

I have been blessed to make *USA Today* twice so far in my career. My last time gracing the list was April 2016. Since then, I have had multiple releases, both within the series that listed and out, and haven't made the cut again. It happens when it happens. Your focus, however, should be a quality original read, not a "title" or crazy amounts of money.

If that's what you're looking for … well, I hope you take disappointment well.

Ryan's Ramblings:

WHEN I READ *Chelsea's Chat* above, all I could think was: *Alright, stop! Collaborate and listen!* If you don't know that song, you're way too young for me, or I'm too old. I'll go with you're young, then I don't feel like the middle-aged woman I am. *Ha!*

Concept—Lord, help us here. When I wrote my first book *Safe*, it sucked. It still isn't the best book I've written, but it's out there, and I take the hits when they come. Why? Because I learned so much from that book. First, I wasn't going to write it. I had just joined this fancy community and loved reading books. I had a shit ton of favorite authors (still do) and read all the time. But I had this story swirling around in my head like a damn tornado.

Some of what happened with Sadie in that book was from my life. It was therapeutic (as was *Needing to Fall*. That'll get anyone cryin'). But I knew nothing. NOTHING. I sucked at English and still do (praise the editors!). I rolled with it and wrote an entire book. Now that I look back, the concept has probably been done many times before and, had I known that at the time, I would have rethought several parts of it.

It was a good story, though; full of suspense and that *holy shit* moment. Now I'd love to go back and redo that book, start from scratch and redo the entire thing. I won't do that, though, because there is no time. That book is out and we roll.

Then I had some people in my life who told me I just *had* to watch *Sons of Anarchy*. I loved MC books at the time, so I figured *what the hell*. I watched five seasons in the course of a few days straight. Yeah, the hubs wasn't too happy with me, but we got past it.

In that show, Gemma and Tara stood out to me. These two strong women, both so damn different. Yet, when it came down to it, not so much. There was one scene where Tara is handing Jax this syringe full of something to kill his stepfather, and she gives Gemma this eye that burned in my head like a razor.

In that moment, Princess was formed in my head. It hit me hard.

Princess isn't like Gemma and Tara, but they were a bouncing off point for me to start. Then, I was a full-time teacher. I started that book during gym time one day while the kids were running around, playing. I still have the paper to this day and will never get rid of it.

It wasn't fan fiction. I wasn't pulling the *Ravage MC* from *SOA*. I made my guys and club totally different. It was just that one scene. One. And it blew me into having to write Princess.

When I wrote that book, it came so damn fast it was crazy. That book sold over 50K copies and has been downloaded free over 150K times. Me, I'll take it.

And it all started with a single scene.

The difference with *Ravage Me* from the preceding books is: I was just excited one person bought my book. I wanted one person to read my book and like it. I wasn't looking at money. I didn't care that I pumped a few grand into the book to get it rolling. I just wanted someone to read it. Then, when a lot of someones started reading it, I got knocked on my ass.

The money didn't matter to me. I was working a full-time job as a teacher and had a good income. But, after its success, I started to get the itch. The itch for more.

Now, for you this could go two different ways. One, you keep your day job and feed that itch. Two, you quit your job and go whole hog. I *highly* recommend that you do not quit your day job! This could end in serious disaster, and you need to seriously talk this through before making that step.

For me, I worked for a full year after *Ravage Me* before I made the decision to pursue writing. Teachers really don't make a whole lot. It's not horrible, but not great, either. My goal was to make my salary in one year writing books. That's it. I didn't need to make a dime more. It was a struggle to make that decision, but I did it. And I'm happy I did.

You need to figure out what you should do for you. What worked for me, may not for you. That's the weird thing about this Indie world ... One never knows for sure.

I'm pretty sure my Ramblings went way off from what Chelsea was talking about. I do that shit a lot.

Coming up with a book concept can be done in so many ways. You could have a spark that ignites the fire under your ass, or you could be one who takes a sheet of paper and just writes every damn topic you can come up with until something sticks out to you.

If you're doing the paper thing, I suggest simplifying it. If you know you don't want to write about sexy firefighters, then don't include them. If you know nothing about sports and aren't feeling like you want to research the hell out of hockey or baseball, don't include it. Instead, make a list of WHAT YOU'RE INTERESTED IN.

Did you catch that, or were the caps not big enough?

You have to be interested in what you write. If you aren't, it's going to show in your writing. It's going to reflect off each page. You're setting yourself up for failure before you even write the first word on that piece of paper or on your computer.

But, Ryan, sports romance is hot, hot, hot right now. I mean, look at the Zon; they're everywhere!

Good for them. You start writing to the trends, you're not going to establish yourself in a genre that you enjoy writing. You want to do that, it's your choice. Personally, I advise against it.

I fell privy to this thinking: *if I just wrote this book, then* bam, *I'll be seen.*

No, it didn't happen. Now, I did write a paranormal series, *The Raber Wolf Pack*, that, let's face it, I'm still trying to earn my money back from in production costs. That book was for me. Yep, plain and simple. I have a hard-on for shifters. Love them. Love the alpha male times a thousand percent. Love being able to create a world where I don't have any rules whatsoever. I love those books. Was it great for my career? Nope. Do I regret it? Nope. Because I enjoyed it.

Don't think I'm contradicting myself here. I had several books out before I wrote the wolves. I had a backlist that was able to hold me pretty well, considering the times. It's all about the risk. The chance. You have to decide if it's for you.

What I'm saying is: find a genre in romance you like writing. Me? Mine's MC Romance. It snowballed, and I enjoy it. There are times that I need a break from it because my already horrible mouth gets even worse and no one needs to listen to that.

If you find an area you love to write, you will have a happier career, because you're doing what you love. It will show in your words and the product you put out there for people's enjoyment.

Money is an evil thing. Don't write a book thinking this book has to make me 15K its first month or in a year. Let's be real. Chances of that happening are super slim, especially if you're a new author and no one has heard of you yet in this world. If you let the money drive you, you'll fall face first on the concrete and get stuck there without breath.

We all want to make a living doing something we love. We all want to have the opportunity to watch our book babies go out there in the world and have others love on them. But you have to remember: *keep it in perspective*. Money isn't going to fall in your lap. This is one of the hardest jobs you'll have. Not only are you writing a novel, you're promoting it, marketing it, setting up tours, cover reveals, finalizing edits, along with writing the next book. It's hard work, and it's not going to happen overnight.

Let me rephrase that …

For most of us, it's not going to happen overnight. As Chelsea said before, it's not a sprint; it's a marathon. I have a bracelet that says this exact saying and wear it a lot. It keeps my perspective in check. What's my end goal? What do I want to accomplish? One look at this bracelet, I get my head back in the game.

Concept Bullet Points

LOOK, this isn't meant to discourage, but if you can't be real with yourself, who can you be real with? This is where you need to be real with you and ask yourself if you can see this through beyond the idea.

The concept of your book needs to be something you're interested in writing. Do not go on the Zon and look up the top selling books and base your decision on what to write from that. No, no, no. Write what *you* enjoy reading. It'll show in your work.

Don't focus on the money. This will only lead to disappointment and accomplishes nothing.

BE YOU! Don't try to be the next big thing. A book will hit, a book will miss. Whatever book you put out there will be attached to your name for all of eternity. Make it a good one.

CHAPTER TWO

FOLLOW THROUGH: THIS IS WHERE YOU ACTUALLY WRITE. I KNOW IT'S HARD, BUT YES, YOU ACTUALLY WRITE!

O kay, your idea is on point. What's next? Write the book!

ASK yourself a few questions before you even get to the first letter of the first word:

1. Are you a planner or a fly by the seat of your pants person? Will you want to follow an outline or write as it comes? Planner or Panster (business terms)?

2. Are you old-school or new-school? Do you want to write and plan with pen and paper? Do you want software to organize your notes? Do you just want to type or use dictation software?

3. Are you into the details or not?

Chelsea's Chat:

TAPS MIC Is this thing on?

You're still with us! Whew, that's a positive. I know this whole Indie world is intimidating, to say the least. Okay, put on your favorite undies and get ready.

Write your book. It's both the easiest and hardest thing you're going to do in this whole process.

I know, I know. CC, you contradicted yourself. Which is it? Hard or easy?

Like I said, both.

Your first book will be the easiest you write because you won't be thinking about what the last reviews said, or about your skillset, or the opinions of your readers (you don't have any yet, not officially). There is a lot less pressure on that first book.

The books I have written the fastest, easiest, and enjoyed the most were *Restore My Heart* (my first ever release), a comic book called *Super Ant* when I was in Ms. Johnson's sixth grade English class, *Merciless Ride* (*Hellions Ride 3*), and *Stay*. I didn't get in my head and worry what anyone was going to think, and the words flowed out of me like magic.

So, it's time to ask yourself some questions. One is: plan or fly by the seat of your pants? Well, that is truly a personal decision. I write faster when I have an outline. I love outlines. It is helpful for series for the way my mind works. That said, I have partners who absolutely despise them (*cough, cough, Ryan, cough*).

I'm gonna be real honest for a second with you. I have a plan for everything. Typically, going into the new year, my entire writing, signing, and vacation schedule for the year is finalized by the fall of the previous year. Like, I have already set my signings for 2018, and we are in April 2017. My writing schedule for this year was nailed out with only one opening available, which I do on purpose in case I have some idea that must be written, or if my health causes me to need a break. I like to have a plan.

My promotions team typically have a plan two months in advance, which helps getting sign-ups and making sure I stay on track. This DOES NOT work for everyone.

If you don't like high pressure situations, then, by all means, DO NOT give yourself some schedule that will make you crack.

I joke constantly that my schedule has a schedule and my outlines have an outline, and it's true. If you like outlines, do it! If you are going to spend hours trying to set one up, only to scrap it, then don't start it in the first place.

Time is money. Don't waste your time. Make sense?

Okay, so you have determined if you're going to have a plan or use your pants. Now, how do you want to execute your writing?

Do you want software that will put the ideas into an outline for you? Do you want a story board? Do you want to use old-school pen and paper? Do you want to open Word and type?

You have to find what you're comfortable with.

Guess what? The first eight books I ever wrote were done completely on pen and paper before I typed the first word. Yes, I handwrote them all. It actually took me forcing myself to type from my outline to break the habit, because I was doing double the work, and time is money. I was wasting time.

Whatever your system, don't be afraid to make changes if you find yourself having writer's block or struggling to stay on task.

This is going to be the hard part: FINISHING the first draft.

Look, hard truth: anyone can write anything. The question is: can you see it through to those magic words *The End*? Do you realize that even writing a story start to finish is an accomplishment in itself even without publishing?

Yes, I have projects on top of projects unfinished. There are some I will never finish. The drive to survive in this industry has to come from inside yourself. No one can give you the go button to make it to the end but yourself. Do it!

Okay, so you found your zone, you found your mojo. Now you need to polish up your manuscript. The time is here. Do you want the details or not? This is a delicate balance between too much and too little. You don't want a reader to start skimming because you give too much, but you don't want to hold back, and then they can't picture the story in their mind.

Go back over your manuscript and make sure you are fleshing out your story to your comfort zone.

Be ready, because the next step is a doozy, and if you haven't gotten real with yourself yet, well, you will drown in what's to come.

This is something I can't say enough. It's a hard truth. Be real with yourself. If you aren't getting honest with you, then you will crumble with what comes ahead.

Ryan's Ramblings:

I'M way different than Miss Chelsea in this area. While she's a planner, I am not. Nope. Hate outlines and would rather choke than make one. I'm what some call a panster. I write by the seat of my pants and see where the book is going to come out. This doesn't work for many people and that's Okay. BE YOU!

When I sit down to write a book, I have this idea in my head. It can come from a song I heard or a movie clip. Really, anything that triggers my brain to get me moving. My latest book, *Bound by Desire*, started with Eminem's "Lose Yourself." On repeat. Over and over and over and over. And, ladies and gents, I don't listen to music while I write. So, I wasn't writing during this time. I had my earbuds in, eyes closed, and let the music pump the shit out of me.

Many of you can write with music thumping through your ears. Me? Nope. I just sing along to the music and totally forget about the book I'm writing. It doesn't work for me.

After listening, I grabbed my computer and just wrote for hours, letting the scenes roll out of me. I had thousands of words in hours. It was fantastic.

With being a panster, though, there are problems. One major one is: not knowing where to go next in your book. Oh, this happens to me so many times it isn't funny. I'll be lying in bed, a story all jumbling in my head, and wake up the next day no better. The next night, I'll go back to bed, and then *BAM*, out of nowhere this thought pops into my head, smacking me so hard I have to get my ass out of my warm bed and get on the computer before it disappears from my head.

This happens all the way through the book because you have no clear direction, as you would were you to have a tangible outline. You'll get to the end of the book and think, *fuck, I forgot to tie this up*. Or, *shit, I totally skimmed over that*. But the thing is, you can have a totally put together outline and still end up with those same results.

I like being a panster because my mind works better that way. I like the flow of the story. I like to live it with my characters. I like to go on their journey with them, not knowing where they are going or what they are doing. I like having that *BAM*, in your face moment and that feeling of exhilaration when it all comes together.

Do I get frustrated? Fuck yeah. There are times when I can't write for days because I'm stuck. No, I'm not an author that can move on from the point I'm at and write another scene from down the road. My brain doesn't like skipping around. Why? Because I have no clue what will happen. That is fun for me. Let's be straight. I get off on that shit. That's the excitement of writing for me.

There are those of you *cough, Chelsea* who have to do outlines. More power to you. I know for a fact that she excels at that shit. Hell, I even tried it, but broke out in hives and needed to burn the paper I wrote on. *ICK!*

You have to find out what works for you. There is NO WRONG way!

Since I'm a panster, I don't have a system to keep notes because, well, I don't need them. It's all in my brain. Now, if I have an idea that pops in my head for later, I will make a comment bubble in my document and toss that information there. Some authors I know use Scrivener.

I have the program and tried it. Personally, it made me anxious. There was so much going on that it made my brain want to scream and run for the hills. I have friends, though, who LOVE that program and use it every day, no matter what.

I do have Excel sheets on my books. Such as the timeline for the Ravage MC series, because that series, all five plus (I say plus because of epilogues and novellas), is all connected in a way I have to know my shit. You start at the beginning, learn there's shit going on, and it carries through the entire series. I'll never do that shit again, because, damn, that was one of the hardest things I've ever had to do. But, I feel accomplished that I got my shit together.

That Excel sheet has been a lifesaver on more than one occasion. I also have an AWESOME reader, Kimberly, who you'll hear about several times in this book from me. She's been making me a Bible. Yep, you heard me. A *Ravage MC Bible*. Places, descriptions, actions—all of it. For each book. It's a LIFESAVER, people. I'm not shitting you. When you have all of your information right there, it makes everything so much easier.

So, no, I don't plan my books, nor have a specific program for my books, but I do have Excel sheets with important information on them.

Schedules. Being a panster, I hate them. My anxiety flies through the roof when I know I have deadlines for things and nothing to produce. I know this. I feel this. Yet, I did it this year. I know! SMH!!! This is my plan for the *Ravage MC Bound Series*. This year, I will have four books in that series released. When one book releases, it will have the preorder links for the next book. When that books goes live, preorder for the next. Catch my drift?

My thinking is: if my readers find the book they just read to be kickass, they're going to want to make sure they have the next one. And so on. In doing this, I put myself on a schedule, because the great god of Amazon will screw you big time if you fuck up those preorder dates. One day late, they'll suspend your ass from preorders and you're fucked. Another reason: you need to be sure about what you're doing.

In doing the every three months' gig, I put myself on a schedule with the *Bound* series and have to float in the other books in three of my other series to close them out this year. It's a lot. At the moment, I'm thinking it's too much since I'm sitting here writing this when I should have my ass working on my book.

Moving on from that.

If that kind of stress is too much for you, don't do it to yourself. Yes, you have a choice. You are your own boss. Let me repeat. YOU ARE YOUR OWN BOSS! You determine your schedule, and if you think it's too much, then it is, and you need to rethink.

Especially if you're doing signings, you need to think about what you're doing. Those suckers are fantastic, but take up a lot of time. Not only packing, getting ready, and attending; but coming home, unpacking, and unwinding. God forbid you get sick in there somewhere. Then, you're screwed.

When you make your schedule, be realistic! You don't have to pump out a book a month. (Believe me; I'm learning this the hard way right now, so don't be me). You don't have to have a book out every two months or three months. Three months is a great goal to have a book out in, but if you can only do one every four, then that will be your max. Meaning you need to plan yourself into writing three books a year. Not everyone can do that schedule, either. Some only write two books a year, or one.

You have to do what you can do. If you drive yourself into the ground, you do neither yourself or your readers any good. Think about it. Analyze it. But don't beat a dead horse either, because your ass needs to be writing.

Follow Through Bullet Points

DO YOU, be you, and find what works for you!

If you're currently writing and you're a planner but find yourself struggling, toss the outline and free yourself from the pressure. If you're a panster and fight writer's block continually, challenge yourself to write an outline and stick to it for one book and see where it goes.

The only thing constant in this book world is there is constant change. If something isn't working, try something else. Yes, it's that simple.

Get into a writing and publishing routine and stick with it.

CHAPTER THREE

EDITING, CRITIQUE PARTNERS, AND BETA READERS, OH MY!: EGO HAS NO PLACE IN EDITING, EVEN IF THEY BOTH START WITH E!

C heck your ego here.

Seriously, do not go any further into this thinking you are the shit and you got this without help from anyone. You are reading this book, so you're obviously looking for something.

All right, now that we have cleared the air.

Hi, my name is Chelsea and my girl, Ryan, and I write books. You are? **Insert your introduction**

WE ARE ALL THE SAME!

Guess what? Ain't nobody (my editor is going to kill me for that one because it's going to stay even after edits because this is self- publishing and we can do that) wrote a first draft that was error proof and the best book ever written, okay?

So, questions:
1. What defines a quality editor to me?
2. Who can I truly see as a critique partner?
3. Beta readers, how many? Why not just my critique partner?

Chelsea's Chat:

I AM the comment bubbling bitch! I own it. I have author friends who I beta read for (Ryan, Jessie Lane, SM Donaldson). If they make a social media post about bubbles or a bubble bitch, it's me they're referring to. I am totally at peace with it. ;)

Look, there is not a more crucial point in your writing than editing. It is a multi-step process. You will need to define your own process because, for each author, it's different. This is mine (please, please, for the love of Pete, understand that this is not what will work for everyone. So, if it doesn't work for you, don't think you did something wrong).

Step one: The light bulb goes on.

I get my best ideas in the car rider line, waiting to pick my kids up from school; in bed after I've been up later than my bedtime—no joke, sleep deprivation turns my brain on—and in the shower. Ryan gets more random texts messages from me with book ideas than she probably cares to get. This little number right here started as a 10 p.m., my time, nine, hers, text message. No shit, real deal. This was a text message before it was anything else.

Step two: Outline.

Now, we have established I love them. My outlines usually are broken down chapter by chapter (this is not for everyone).

Step three: Blurb.

Again, I can't say it enough. This is not for everyone. I happen to love writing blurbs. I'm a tease (ask my high school boyfriend. I own that shit. lol). I write my blurb right behind my outline. A lot of authors write the blurb after the book is completed. That's okay, too. I just love them so, like a junkie looking for a fix, I go in balls to the walls.

Step four: Write.

Okay, so I'm going to break off the steps for a moment to explain something that intercedes. I begin writing and usually will do the opening five chapters before anyone else sees my work (unless it's a co-written book, and well, peeps, that is a whole different ball game we can dive into in another edition). Now that I have my opening, it goes to my critique partner (some people will wait to use critique partners and betas until the story is complete).

IT TAKES A VILLAGE! This is the section where you learn you can't do this shit on your own.

Step five: Write and Critique.

Multitask? What, what! Yes, I keep writing while I anxiously await my superhero bitch to fix my opening shit. I'm going to disappoint you here because I am not going to reveal my critique partner's identity, but I have one, and she gets my work before anyone else.

Okay, I'm adding this note after the fact since, yeah, Ryan Michele is my superhero. But she's mine, and I don't share well. Sorry, not sorry, but real deal, she gets my work before anyone else and the email literally *says rip it.*

A critique partner needs to be someone you trust. They get your work before a copyright can be placed on the material, so please do NOT ever put out an open invitation for beta readers or critique partners. A critique partner needs to be someone who will not spare your feelings. Yes, I said it. *They need brass fucking balls!* And you, my friend, kiss your feelings goodbye.

It's not personal. Your critique partner is there to polish your work and make you see your vision with different glasses on. This is critical in making your work the best it can be. If you have beta readers and a critique team that only tell you good things ... well, they need to be fired, even though they don't get paid.

Hard truth: nobody gets shit right the first time. There will ALWAYS be something to tweak.

I would rather my critique partner hand me my ass before I send my book baby into the world and get nailed in reviews. Thicken your skin, put on your best bra, whatever you need to hold yourself up, but find someone not afraid to rip your shit apart.

Please note: this is not an invitation to ask myself or Ryan to critique your work or beta read for you. While I do critique for some close author friends, it is not something either of us have time in our schedules for, and quite honestly, I have to have a bond with someone to be able to really be honest about their work to the level I expect in a critique partner. I am super sensitive about hurting feelings of people not in my inner circle. And, well, those in my circle get me no holds barred. It's a bond and a place I have to be with someone. It's nothing personal. Really, it's not you; it's me.

I want you to find your own team and comfort levels. And I would like to add, if a partner or beta reader isn't working out for you, then it's okay to cut them loose ... politely. I have been fired on more than one occasion as a beta reader or critique partner. It happens. I promise, I didn't lose sleep over it, and I didn't get my feelings hurt.

Feelings are for inside the pages, not in the edits. You get me?

So, you see, a critique partner is the raw reader for you. After you find the hardest hardass to be your first go-to, then you set yourself up with beta readers.

Now, there are differing opinions on a beta's job. Let me be clear. The materials in this book are simply the experiences and opinions of myself and Ryan Michele. Therefore, if you see things differently, that is OKAY! And you will find in some topics Ryan Michele and I have differing opinions or views, and it's so totally normal.

All right, whew, that's a load off.

I see beta readers as readers. My beta readers are just that. In fact, my closest ones don't blog, they don't write, they have nothing to do with the industry. They aren't my family. I didn't even know who they were until they read my books and we met in an online group. I do have some author friends who beta read for me because having another author with similar editing experiences helps to see my work in a different view to clean it as much as I can. I have bloggers on my team, as well. It's about who I can mesh with, and frankly, who isn't scared to tell me when my shit sucks or doesn't make sense because, guess what? Sometimes it does.

Step six: After I fix what my critique partner says and send off the next section to be shredded (legit, that's what I send in the email. *Shred me, rip me, tell me all the bad things* are just a few examples for ya), I have my betas go over that opening.

This process is repeated usually five chapters at a time until I complete the work. Then we move on to my editors.

Yes, I said it plural. I have more than one editor, and this is why it costs cake to produce a book.

Quality editors cost money. Bottom line: if you need to save money, do not save it on your editor. Editing should be your biggest expense.

Let me be very clear here. Book editing is not just about having a degree in English or Literature. There are multiple steps in editing. Copy edits, line edits, content edits—you need it all.

Step seven: Editing.

I'm not going to preach anything more, other than to say: do your research, find an editor you can blend with, and pay them without delay, because they damn sure deserve it. At the end of this book, we will provide a list of editors, including the ones we use, or have heard positive things about. What you choose is on you, but an editor is a critical element to your finished product.

For over three years now, I have been in tight with Kris from *C&D Editing*. Hands down, I don't feel comfortable with a release unless I have Kris at least get one read through, but most times, we have two because I love the work she does and being able to release with the confidence in my edits. I have used Asli from *E.L. Editing* as well.

Asli is my very first editor, and we both have grown so much together in the last four years. She gets all my work as my final proofreader after I finish first and second edits. And, depending on my struggles in the writing process, she sometimes is part of my first and second edits, meaning she goes through my work sometimes three to four times before the final goes out. I am not good with grammar and have never claimed to be.

The strongest editor I have ever worked with is Pam from *Bulletproof Editing*, but she books well in advance and I usually can't get a lock on the right timing for us to work together consistently, but I truly respect her time, her work, and her input.

I am what's known as a hybrid author, so I also have to deal with multiple editors inside my publishing house with my traditionally published books. That is not for this book, as the process with traditional publishing is quite different from my self-publish process.

Step eight: Face the edits.

Edits are ugly. No one likes them. I cry. Yes, I literally cry every time I get edits back. It happens. Then, guess what? After those edits are finished, they go for another round based on changes.

I don't cry because my shit is messed up. No, I cry because I get mad that I still missed shit. I mean, come on; do you realize how many times I have gone over these words? But the thing is, like that commercial for air scent stuff that says you go nose blind, I go word blind. That's what I call it. It happens. So, when you get your edits back, know you are not alone in the emotions it will bring out in you.

Step nine: Proofing.

Just like having a quality editor, you need a solid proofreader. What gets missed because track changes doesn't save something or something is mixed up, your proofer is there to catch. I promise you the cost of the additional proof pays off rather than dealing with reformatting your book multiple times, especially if you don't handle your own formatting. Then you will pay money each time you need to fix something. Do it right the first time so you don't have to go back.

I made a ton of mistakes in my first series, and now I have spent the money and the time to redo them, from covers, edits, and formatting, all to make sure I am giving the best work to my readers, and that includes all of my backlist.

So, this is how I get from concept to finals. You will find your own system in time and what works for you. If something isn't working or it's a time sucker, then change it. The beautiful thing about being Indie is that you make your own path.

Ryan's Ramblings:

WHEW! I'm not even sure where to start here!

My process of writing a book. Holy hell, you may want to get another Diet Coke, or coffee and some snacks. This one's gonna be long.

You need editors. There is no question about it. If you don't have an editor, you need to wait until you can afford one. Some editors do payment plans, and that's something to definitely look into. But note: they won't give you your manuscript back until your shit's paid in full. They've put a lot of work into your book and want their cash. Can't blame them for that.

What does this mean? Plan it out early. If your editor will let you break it down weekly and you can pay a chunk during a four-week period, then you need to balance your schedule as such. As in, that book needs to be ready to roll the week of that third payment and at the editor's, so when you make that fourth payment, you have your book to put out there. Not all editors do payments, though.

A lot of editors charge by the word. Such as $0.004 per word. Therefore, you have a document with 50,000 words, you're looking at, at least, $200, and you need to budget that. Some charge more than this, much more, so you need to be prepared for that cost. It can run you up to $800, depending on the editor you choose. Some charge by the page, as well. Make sure you do your homework and find this information out before it's time to send off your book baby.

I've gone through several editors in my time as an author. Either we didn't click, or I just didn't have the right feel for some of them. This is fine. You're human, and you need to be comfortable with who you are paying to work on your baby. If you don't, how can you trust what they say when they rip your shit to shreds?

Let's get into my process before I get carried away and become a chatterbox.

Step one: *Ding, ding, ding, we have a winner!*

I'm a panster, so my ideas hit me at all different times. What I've come to realize now is that a bulk of them come while I'm lying in bed before I close my eyes. For me, this sucks. One, because I want to hightail my ass out of bed and get to my computer. Two, because I can't stop thinking about it and barely sleep as the wheels in my head begin to turn.

What I've done is keep a pad of paper by my bedside and a pen. That way, in the middle of the night, when I'm having this huge-ass epiphany, I can jot it down so I don't forget. I'm old and forget shit. A lot! If I don't write it down, I'm fucked. I've tried just getting up in the morning and letting it rip … just to hear crickets.

Step two: *Pull out the clicker and get to pushin'.*

Start writing. It can be a sentence or two; it can be an entire chapter. Whatever it is that hits you, get it down. Get those thoughts going and get the start up to your book flowing.

During this process, at the beginning, I keep to myself. It's usually not until the first 10K do I even show it to my critique partner to shred to pieces. And yes, I want her to shred it, dismember it, destroy it. This brings me to the next step.

Step three: *10K or bust!*

Your critique partner needs to be someone you trust wholeheartedly. You're giving them your baby, entrusting they will take care of it. Yes, you want them to completely decimate it, but it's still your baby. BUT! you DO NOT want a critique partner who is going to stroke your back and tell you what an awesome, fantastic person you are. No. No and no!

Also, a critique partner is NOT a beta reader!!! You must learn the difference between the two. A critique partner is normally another author, but is not limited to, who picks apart your manuscript piece by piece. While a beta reader isn't as harsh. There is a difference, so you know what to expect.

Well, Ryan, how the hell do I find me one of those? Good question. It's hard as hell. Personally, I've been fired from several authors because my bubbles are harsh. I'm not trying to be a bitch at all. What I'm trying to do is grab those little inconsistences that one reader will read six months from now and slam you for it on a review. I'm not there to be someone's best friend. I'm here to help your story grow.

It's no surprise that Chelsea and I are partners in this sense. She has thick skin when it comes to me shredding her shit. And I do. Harshly. Because I want what's best for her. Because I want be a help to her and not a hindrance. If I were to tell her that her book had only two small issues, she'd tell me flat-out I was full of shit. Because she's right. Normally, on the first page, I make anywhere from five to twenty comment bubbles. On the first page. Yep, shred, baby.

So, let's get back to where you can find your shredder. I like that name better. I'm gonna start calling Chelsea that. Makes her sound badass.

Engaging in the book community is where you're going to find your shredder. Now, if you're just starting out, you may just have a beta reader to start and have to work yourself up (And believe me; you can find betas who do just as great of a job as a shredder). When you first start out and have no reader base whatsoever, you ask your mother, sister, best friend, Aunt Wilma, or Betsy down the road who read a book once in her life. Yep, we have to start somewhere, people.

Each person who reads it will have a different opinion, and in some way will help you enhance your story. Will you find that shredder from your mom? Nope. You're perfect and wonderful and sunshine shoots out of your ass when it comes to her. But she will help you if there are serious things wrong with the book. Most likely. Now, you could have a mom that is totally the opposite of this wanting to bring you down, if that's the case, I wouldn't have her on your list of readers because you won't know if it's true and honest.

Do you know anyone in the book world? A blogger? Another reader. Chances are, if you decided to become an Indie romance author, you're in this world in some way, shape, or form.

Most people don't wake up out of the blue, never having read a book before, and say, *damn I'm gonna be an author!* Therefore, you have to know someone. You may not get the results you were intending right away, but let me tell you, there are some kickass bloggers out there who will rip your shit and leave your mouth hanging open. I love it.

I will not sit here and give you names. Why? Because those are my relationships that I've built over time. They are trusted, cared for, and developed. You need to find that for you.

There are paid services for beta readers, as well. Now, I personally don't pay my people, except in signed paperbacks if they would like them, and lots of hugs. You, if you don't have any avenue to go to, can pay for this service. Most of the time, they are editors who give you a lower price to read through your manuscript. But this is another cost that you will need to budget out for.

Step four: *Recycle, Repeat, Fix, Scream, Keep Going.*

This stage, I'm chugging along writing my book. My girl has shredded and bubbled up my first 10K, and I'm going back in, fixing, screaming, and moving the fuck on. Once I hit the 20K mark. I send it back to Chelsea, and she does her thing. I repeat my shit and do my thing again.

This is where beta readers come in for me, about the 20K mark of a book. Even being a panster, I have a pretty good grasp of the characters, their personalities, faults, and triggers. So, I ship my baby off to my beta readers.

I have several of these. You need several of these. As you grow your reader base, they'll be easier to find. If you have a couple of books under your belt, you ask those readers. You do this through your Facebook reader group (yes, you need one of these. If you don't have one, put this book down and march your ass to FB and create one now). When I first started doing betas back in the day, I made a Google doc. The many things on the Google doc were: if they'd ever read my books before, having them provide links to their reviews and answering a few questions. A main point you must make is that they will not pirate or share your book in any way. Yes, you need to do this. I also recommend having them sign a non-disclosure agreement. Or, at least on the sign-up doc, have a question there they have to answer that states they won't share.

Sift through those who show interest, then give them the first chapter of your manuscript. I know! Don't hyperventilate. Have them use Microsoft Word track changes; let them do their thing. Give them a couple of days for this. Then evaluate.

Look for those people who caught something important. Not the misspelled words, because if it were me, that'd take for-fucking-ever. You want the ones who caught the man had blond hair when you started, but by the end of chapter, he had dark hair that blows in the wind it's so long.

You want that reader who is going to see the man went from sitting back with his hands behind his head to miraculously standing over at the window, gazing out of it.

You want to see if your beta made comment bubbles and what each of those say. For example, did they make a comment like: *this sentence is choppy and makes no sense with what you're trying to convey here*? Or does it say something like: *Don't get it*? Do you see the difference in those two comments? One gives you a direction, while the other has you asking: *okay, what didn't you get?* Know the difference and know what you are looking for. It does you no good to hand your book over to someone who's not going to help you fix those problems.

Step five: *The blurb from hell.*

I don't know about you, but I fucking hate blurbs. Like, just pull my nails out, hate them. It is the bane of my existence when it comes to a book. And since I'm a panster, I normally wait until the book is pretty well done before I write the blurb since I have no clue what's going to happen in the story. Lucky for me, I have Chelsea, who helps me with this shit so I'm not horribly far behind the curve. I mean *Bound by Desire* is up for preorder, not written, and it's got a blurb!

I feel like I could write an entire section on blurb writing. Hell, I could probably write, like, four of them in actuality.

Your blurb has to pull readers in. You have only seconds of a reader scanning those first two to four lines of that blub to hook them. You don't, they are lost in the wind. It has to have punch. It can't give too much away, yet it needs to give the reader an idea of the journey you are taking them on.

Write it. You'll delete it many, many times and write it again. Then start to tweak it. Send it to your critique partner and let them shred it. Fix it. Send it to beta readers and see what they say. Fix it. If you have a reader group, post it in there and ask them their opinions. Fix it. Send it to your friend in Texas who reads. Fix it. You keep doing this until you're happy with what you have.

There are paid services for this, as well. I have yet to use them, but have seriously thought about it. There's one called *Blurb Bitch*. I haven't used her, but her concept is intriguing. A big thing with these is that you've gotta be alright with losing some of the control. If you hire someone to do the job, you need to accept what they come up with. If you hate it, there's no rule book that says you have to use it. BUT, you're out the cake and time. Always think about this.

Step six: *Write, bitch, write!*

Now is the time to get that book finished. This is a mixture of the above time. It's where I write, send it to critique, fix, send it to a beta. Over and over again until it's where I want it. The trick with this for me is that I do them individually. This takes time. If you want to do it this way, you need to plan for your team members—because, let's face it, you're all a team—to have time to read and write up comments.

For me, I do Chelsea. She reads and shreds. I fix. Then I send it to one beta. She reads and comments. I fix. Then I send it to another beta. She reads and comments. I fix. I keep doing this several times. After my team has done their thing, it's my turn.

Step seven: *Read it again, woman!*

Start at page one and read every single word you typed. Some like to print out their manuscript and do it with a pen and paper. I've done this before, but my problem is it takes up so much time. Because, not only am I making the marks on paper, I then have to go back in the document and fix the issues. Me, I like to kill two birds with one stone. I do it on my laptop. Fix the problems as I go. Sometimes after I read it, I start back at page one and read it again. Yep.

This is the shit you need to know. I've heard authors say, *I can't read my own work.* Why? You wrote it. You want it to be the best possible product you can put out there for your readers. You want it to shine, sparkle, and dance so readers will choose you in a sea of many. If this is you, personally, I don't get it, but I don't have to. You need to figure out what your next step is at this point.

Me? I'm reading.

Step eight: *You thought your critique partner knew track changes? She ain't got shit on your editor.*

Yeah, this shit's scary. No sugar coating it at all. The first time I got edits back on my first book, I cried. Bawled like a damn baby. Why? Because my precious baby that I sent to the editor was now covered in so many marks that it was ruined. Destroyed. And I'd just done everything I possibly could to make it the best book possible. This was *Safe*, and we had a moment.

When I sent *Ravage Me* in, I knew it would be the shit. I wouldn't have any of those dingy little marks that said I spelled this or that wrong. I wouldn't have bubbles that told me there were plot holes because I worked my ass off to make it so perfect that she couldn't find a damn thing.

POP! What was that you ask? My bubble bursting into a million pieces and shattering all over the damn place. This book had more bubbles, more marks, more fuck-ups that needed fixing. Except, this time, I didn't cry. Why? Because I knew I could fix them. Just like I did before. I learned from my first book how to make things work, how to fix them, how to change them and make them better.

I wasn't going in blind.

That first edit you get back will hurt. The second, not so much. The third, you're like: *bring it*. The fourth: *is that all you've got?* The fifth: *oh, you can do better than that …* And it continues. Now, it's sick, but I enjoy seeing as many marks as I possibly can because each of those marks is making my book stronger, better, and giving my reader the experience that I want them to have while reading my book.

It's all in the perspective you have on the process. Have a positive one, you'll stay positive. Keep that dread, you'll sink.

Step nine: *Fix the bitch again and ship it off to proof! Poof!!!*

Fixing edits isn't fun for me. Some authors love it. Me? It's not my favorite part of the process, but it's not horrible, either. With my editor, Kris from *C&D Editing*, she does the edits, I go back in and fix, then I have the opportunity for her to go through again. The last couple of books I haven't done that because **high five** she said I didn't need it. BUT, I do a full read through again after edits.

I do use a proofreader after my final read through, though. It's that extra set of eyes that looks through each sentence of your work just in case. I use Silla Webb from *Masque of the Red Pen*, and it'll cost ya. Just like my editor will cost ya. You need to make sure you've budgeted for that money and have it ready to pay or you won't get your precious book back until you do.

After my final proof, the book is ready for formatting. Damn, that's a long-ass process, and I'm sure I missed some shit in there.

Editing Bullet Points

HIRE PROFESSIONAL, QUALITY EDITORS!

Know what a quality editor means to you. For me, they need experience, and they need to be qualified with both education and experience.

Find editors you are comfortable with and take care of them. Meaning: pay them for their services. They are worth it.

Decide what you want in beta readers and critique partners, and assemble your team.

CHAPTER FOUR

COVER DESIGN: EVERYONE WILL HAVE AN OPINION AND NONE OF THEM ARE RIGHT!

S hit's gonna get deep here.

QUESTIONS TO ASK:
1. What do I want the story to convey?
2. What's my budget?
3. Does my name stand out on the cover?

Chelsea's Chat:

I WANT to take a moment to be very clear here. The following opinions are MY own. They are not intended to offend anyone.

Okay, let me be frank with you ... I hate covers! Yes, I said it. My very favorite cover is black with gold letters, the Holy Bible.

This book here, the one you're reading, is not the Bible of anything. Regardless, I absolutely hate covers. All of them.

There isn't a single cover of mine that I could say is my favorite. I just don't like covers. However, there are people who love them. My dear friend, Author Tracie Redmond, is a self-proclaimed cover whore. She loves covers. She is very honest with me when she doesn't like mine. I respect her opinion.

You should also know that when it comes to covers, everyone is going to have an opinion.

Okay, so how can I help you when I hate covers. Well, I can keep shit simple.

Your mindset is what will get you through this writing world from beginning to end. Your mindset on a cover needs to focus on a few key things; the rest is irrelevant. Yes, I said it.

Your cover is your visual representation of your book, your story. Make sure it fits. Do not put some inked up, badass on a cover of some preppy boy's love story.

This is where things are going to get me in trouble, but I want to be real. Do not put a model on your cover because you want them to promote your book. I absolutely adore *Furious Fotog*. Working with Golden is amazing. But my work is my work, and it needs to represent me and my story, not the model on the cover or the photographer who took the picture.

Now, I will say that working with Golden, Eric Battershell, Cassy Roop, and many more has been amazing. I have both purchased individual pictures from their stock libraries and had a custom shoot with a model and Golden. Top notch work, so this is a viable way to really make sure your vision for your cover is on point. My custom shoot, Golden nailed the shot I was looking for in the first ten minutes.

I just want to be clear that you should not seek out a model or photographer because you think it will get your work seen. The book is a package deal, okay? It's everything coming together and needs to match.

You also want to make sure the people you choose to work with are professional at all times. Do not get your work caught up in the crossfire of some social media nightmare because someone happens to be on your cover or tied to your cover and they do something rude. You are in control of your career. Don't let it be impacted or affected by the actions of someone else all because of a cover.

Okay, so question two: budget.

Photographers and models deserve to get paid! Let me be clear, they are providing their time, their service, their talent, and just like you, should get paid for your book. They should get paid for their contribution.

If you don't have money for a custom shoot or picture from a photographer, please know there are stock photo sites. I use them for covers, as well. But I want to be clear: read your fine print.

You must purchase the proper license for a cover. Some sites are set up only to be able to give you digital-only prints, meaning you could never use your cover on a paperback. Furthermore, there are some photos that will be for editorial use or can't be modified. If the picture doesn't give the license to grant permission to be cropped, used in print, or altered, guess what? You can't use it.

One of the quickest ways to get sued in this business—outside of plagiarism—is to use a picture for your cover without proper authorization.

THIS GOES FOR TEASERS AS WELL!

You can't simple google a picture and download it. You must retain the rights to use the image, period. Make sure you have your shit tight. Do not even chance that no one will find it because you are not known. Be upstanding in your work and reputation.

So, you have a cover picture, what next? Well, you can design your own cover if you're good with graphics. I'm not patient enough.

There are some great cover designers out there. I use Marisa from *Cover Me Darling* the most, but I have also had great results from *IndieVention Designs*, Mina Carter, and Jessie Lane.

My one day dream come true is to have a cover designed by Sarah Hansen of *Okay Creations*.

If there is nothing else you can take away from this book, please take this:

YOUR NAME IS YOUR BRAND!

Okay, why am I so stuck on your name on your cover? Because your backlist is where your consistent money is going to come from and will keep your career level. So, that being said, your name is everything. Make it stand out.

I want to remember the author more than I want to remember the sexy cover.

This also means on your teasers, make your name *pop*. **And your social media behavior will be your name, so make sure you keep your shit tight in every aspect.** I am not going to get into my thoughts of authors behaving badly, other than to say: that's your name. What do you want people to say who follow it? I want mine to be: *Chelsea Camaron is a straight up broad who makes me feel with every book she writes.*

Really, ask yourself: what do you want your name, your brand to be? Then make it show.

Ryan's Ramblings:

BLAH! Yep, that's how I'm starting the cover discussion. Why? Because they're hard for me. I don't have that artistic eye that some have, though I wish I freaking did. When I see something, I need to see it pretty much finished in order for my brain to compute. This goes for photos used for covers as well. I have several photos from photo shoots that are sitting on my laptop, not being used. I know, it's terrible! But they ended up not fitting what I wanted to do for the book. I was lucky where I wanted to use one for one book, I ended up using another, and then the original ended up being used for another. It was a win-win!

Over the years, I've worked with several cover designers. Melissa Gill from *MGbookcovers* created all the awesomeness that is the *Ravage MC* series.

When I started writing that series, it was just for fun people. I had no clue readers would like it and want more. I had no idea that one book would start my path to a different life than the one I was living. *Nada.*

Melissa had a vision with the black, gray, whites, and reds. I loved those colors and rolled with it. Like I said, I'm not a cover gal. No clue over here, people. I went with her vision and am happy I did. Not only did she start the BRANDING of the *Ravage MC* series, she started my branding as an author.

Has my branding changed over the years? Yep, sure has. But it was a starting off point, and we all need to have that.

Cassy Roop from *Pink Ink Designs* came up with the *Vipers Creed* series and the *Ravage MC*

Bound series. Kickass covers. She does a phenomenal job. She's also a photog and does fantastic pics!

I have a new series that will be coming out later in the year at some point, and Susan Garwood from *Wicked Women Designs* made those covers. They don't have the red theme in them, but that's because they're not bikers etc. Love them. Stay tuned to see those.

For the *Ruthless Rebels* series I co-write with Chelsea, *IndieVention Design* made those.

As you can see, I have a wide range of people that I use at any given time. Each one brings something different to the table, and as long as my end product is what I want, we're golden.

When you are doing a cover of a book, you need to keep the number of people outside of you and your designer limited for help. This is just my opinion, from my experience. Why am I saying this? Because opinions are like assholes— everyone has them. You ask ten different people what they think about your cover, you're going to get ten different answers. This is, if those people are being honest with you and aren't there to stroke your ego.

Since we're keeping this raw and real … I've fucked up a few times when it's come to covers. Oh, yeah. Big time. I have sunk a huge amount of money into redoing covers repeatedly. Like, hated the redo, so I did a redo of the redo. Yeah, it's seriously no joke. But this is all on me, totally and utterly, and I take that hit full throttle.

When I started, I was full-out stupid to branding. Branding your name, your books, your career—all of it was an illusion to me that was so far out of reach. I just wanted to write, express myself. All those fun things. Then it starts to turn real. What I'm saying is: you need to know what your branding is going to be.

Let's take me for example. The *Ravage MC* series is black, white, gray, and reds (Thank you, Melissa). I released *Ravage Me* in early 2014. There is no way now I'd go back and rebrand myself with another color. Those are mine. Plain and simple. I'm happy with that. But when I'm doing a cover, I have to keep those colors in mind. All of my bikers and mafia have those colors, except for the *Ruthless Rebels* since that's a co-write. My lighter books, the contemporary ones, are just that—lighter, fluffier, and lots of colors. My wolves have … well, wolves on the covers. The new series that'll be coming out is in blues. *Wait, what?* Yeah, you heard me. The answer to your question is: they are billionaire books. They aren't raw, gritty, bloody, or in your face. There are no zip ties in these books (if you read any of my bikers, you'll know that my favorite thing to use are zip ties. They're so damn easy).

For me, I needed to separate that. The billionaires are something I wanted to write. Just like my wolves back when. I'm doing these boys for me. If readers like them, fantastic. I hope they will, but I can't expect my readers to just flip from my raw, real to alpha no blood. I get that. But this is what happens when you have all those voices that play in your head as a panster and you get deviated from your writing. I also have a strong back list that helps support me while I take these risks. You need to evaluate what's best for you and your career.

Bottom line is: all of my covers, when put together, fit in different categories. Now, if you only have one category, then you don't have to really think so hard about all of this shit. Me, I do. However, you will need to think of future books and how you're going to tie them all together. There is an entire section I could write on branding, but the big thing is: YOUR NAME!

Do you catch that?

YOUR NAME IS YOUR BRAND.

Do I need to say that again? No? Alrighty. Whatever you decide to have on the cover, whether it be a hot guy, couple, stock photo, etc., your name needs to pop out of the cover. If you look at my *Vipers Creed* series or my *Bound by Family* series, you will see my name. Big, bold letters on the bottom. *Vipers*. You really see that shit.

Your name is everything. Yes, you paid a shit ton of money for that awesome photo. Yes, you don't want to totally cover it up. Yes, you want your title and name to pop off the page. If that means covering some of that photo up, you'll need to do it. There is no sense in having a cover with your name the size of newsprint on it. Readers can't read that.

Readers want to look at that thumbnail on the Zon and see who that book is from. If you've BRANDED yourself well, this will be an easy thing.

Let's talk a minute about the awesome photogs I've worked with over the years and a bit about price. Photogs and models are doing a job for you. I know CC stated this above, but it needs to be reiterated. You have to pay them. There is no choice. They are providing a service to you. If you want that service, you pay for it. It's not cheap. No. You want a kickass picture, though, you're going to fork over the cash for it.

You need to decide if it's in your budget to do this. I've bought exclusive covers from anywhere between $450 - $900 before and a wide range between that. Like I said, it's a lot. And you need to have it in your budget if you want to go this route. The photogs get their fee, and the models get theirs. If you have a couples shot, you're going to pay more money because you're paying two models.

Some photogs will let you pay in installments, but I'm not sure if they will allow you to have the cover photo until the amount is paid in full. You'll have to check with each individual photog on this. And straight up, some photogs have gotten so burned before, they won't allow you to do payments. It's in full, or you don't get the picture. You want it bad enough, you'll do what they ask. It's their business that you are trying to get a service from.

Contracts! Contracts! Contracts!!! Each photo you get from a photog should have a contract with it. EACH PHOTO YOU GET FROM A PHOTOGRAPHER SHOULD HAVE A CONTRACT WITH IT! This protects all the parties involved, from the photog, models to you. It also gives you the terms and conditions for which the photograph can be used. Each photog is DIFFERENT!!!

I know I'm capping things a lot here, but I want you to be able to see this. It's important that you read these contracts. If you have a question, ask it! The photographers aren't going to bite your hand when you ask. They want to see the picture as much as you want to buy it. Most of them will work with you, as well.

For example, I wanted to have it in my contract that I could use the photo for audio books, as well. It was added to the contract.

Straight up, the best contract I've seen personally is from Eric Battershell. He gives you exclusive rights to the photo you buy. What are exclusive rights? You own that photo. Full-out, no strings attached. You want to make a blanket with that cover on it and sell it, you can. Most photogs don't offer this. If you make some type of merchandise with their photo on it, you have to pay them a percentage. All of this needs to be worked out before you create said merchandise because that just ends up to be a fuck of a mess.

Wander Agiar Photography is fantastic to work with, too. These are the ones I asked for the changes in the contract, and they were happy to work with me. I had tons of questions, and each one was answered professionally and timely. So much so, I bought three pictures from him in the last couple of months for the *Ravage Bound* series. They are so smoking hot. It's taking everything in my power to keep them a secret.

I've also used Shauna Kruse for two of my photos. One was out of her stock (this means she already had a shoot planned with this model, and I picked a picture from that shoot), and the other was a custom shoot. Her custom shoots come with your cover photo and nine pictures you can use for teasers or swag.

Most photographers have different deals for custom cover shoots. Sometimes it's better to get a custom shoot done, instead of picture from their stock so you can put your stamp on it. These are all things you need to take into account when deciding what you should do since these shoots are going to cost more because of their time, travel expenses, etc.

I've also bought photos from Sara Eirew who has a kickass studio. She has a lot of couple shots, which is what I look for because all my *Ravage* and *Ravage Bound* series are on them. Highly recommend you checking her out, too.

I have personally used all of these photogs for the covers of my books and adore all of them. There are many other photogs out there—look until you find what you need for the cover. You're spending big bucks, so make sure it's what you want and need for your cover.

Whew! That was a lot, and I've only touched on things!

Back to cover design. That is what this section is about, right? *CC!!! Help! I've veering!* I do this a lot, so bear with me.

If you do not want to spend the big bucks for a professional photo, give stock photos a shot. Several of my books have stock. *Ravage Me* for example! Yep, sure does, and I'm not changing it. Read above what CC says about the licensing and stuff. That's important to have in your mind.

Cover designers can make fantastic covers out of stock. Always remember that. If you don't have it in your budget for a professional picture, it's Okay!

Let's talk pre-made covers. I've purchased several of these. I have two, I believe, on standby from Cassy Roop at *Pink Ink Designs;* and one, I believe, from Susan Garwood at *Wicked Women Designs.* Have you joined their groups on Facebook? You should. They post premade covers all the time for a reduced price compared to their custom covers. I'm a member of several different groups. Cassy is in with two other designers, and it's called *Premades 4 Authors.* Susan is *Wicked Women Designs.* You should join and see what they have. Something may jump out at you. Prices range and are reasonable. Be on the lookout for sales. Yes, sales!

Most of the time, with premade covers, you can change the fonts, colors of fonts, and that's about it. Some may let you do a little more, but if you want a lot changed, you'll have to pay for a full design redo of that premade. It's how the world works.

For someone who covers aren't her thing, I sure did yap a lot. I know there's a shit ton of information in a short time. Hope it's all making sense to you.

Cover Design Bullet Points

YOUR NAME IS YOUR BRAND; make it stand out.

Read your licenses. Know what you can and cannot legally do with a photo.

Have a contract if using a model and photographer. Be clear in what you can and can't do, and what you can expect from them in the promotions department.

CHAPTER FIVE

FORMAT: IF YOU DON'T HAVE PATIENCE, THEN YOU BETTER HAVE DOLLARS!

S o, you have that final manuscript, what the hell do you do with it?

QUESTIONS TO ASK YOURSELF:
1. Do I have patience?
2. Do I have cake? (cake is money if you haven't caught on yet)

Ryan's Ramblings:

FORMATTING IS A CHUNK OF CHANGE. It's a pain in the ass. Yet, it's everything when you finish your baby and put it in front of people to read. You've put so much blood, sweat, and tears into this book, why on earth would you put crappy look in front of readers' faces??? Do you need to have fancy schmancy? Nope. But you need to have it look professional.

There are two options when it comes to formatting.

One: you figure out how to do it on your own.

Two: you hire a master to do their work.

For me, I now do all my ebook formatting through Vellum. It's a program through MAC computers that is super, super, super easy. Not going to lie, when Chelle Bliss told me it was easy, I thought she'd lost her mind. Because *hello!* it's formatting. At first, I thought I was getting into a mess of hurt, but for me, it works great. It's taken a learning curve, though. Just recently, I figured out how to add graphics as chapter headers, which adds a unique edge to my books.

The ease of this program is outstanding. It is mostly a copy and paste procedure for the entire book. What I like about it, mostly, is I can easily go back in and fix those boo-boos that we all have once we send out the ARCs to readers. Some may be large problems and others small. With Vellum, I can go in, fix the problem, and upload the new doc ASAP. I'm not waiting for the formatter to fit me in to make those changes and paying the costs for those changes. Me, I can do them at one in the morning and be done. Bottom line, Chelle was right, and I thank her for that little tidbit of information.

Some authors format through Word. I've done this. It's not bad for ebooks, but it is a shit ton more difficult than Vellum. When using Word and transferring it over to .mobi or epubs, I use Calibre. It's a simple way to convert your books.

I've had problems with this, though, because once I convert them from a Word doc, sometimes graphics or italics don't move over to the .mobi file and I have to redo it. It becomes a bit time consuming, but it is possible!

I'm sure there are other programs out there for ebook formatting, I'm just sharing with you what I use and why.

Paperbacks … *Ugh!* Those little shits are the Devil reincarnate! No, I'm not overexaggerating. I'm not so patiently waiting for Vellum to come up with a paperback version of their program, which a little birdy told me is this summer. Until then, I'm using Word. I went on the Createspace website and got their handy dandy template. Word to the wise: that shit's fucked up. If you change that template at all, you change the entirety of the book and have to go back and redo it. It's not easy, and I had to fight Word a thousand different ways.

This happened to me with *Bound by Family*. I spent days formatting that paperback and wanted to throw my laptop several times. Luckily, I didn't, or I'd have been even more pissed at myself. It took asking for help from some kickass author friends to get my shit sorted.

It's not perfect. Nope, not at all. Is it awesome? Yep. Do I love it? Yep. Am I changing it? Nope.

It's personal preference, and you need to make that decision for you.

Hiring the awesomeness that is a formatter, be ready to hand over some cash. There are some very, *very* reasonable formatters out there, but you're looking at, at least, a hundred bucks, give or take. They have fantastic programs and can do some kickass things. For example, Cassy Roop from *Pink Ink Designs*, she did the formatting for the *Vipers Creed* series. She put this AWESOME imprint of a motorcycle on all the chapter pages. Now, my Word doc isn't going to do that, because I have no clue where to start with that. Is it awesome? Hell yes! Will she be doing the last book in that series? Yes! Is the fact that I'm doing my own now a reflection of her? Absolutely NOT!!!

I wanted to do my own for two reasons. One, I'm a creative bug and like to learn new things. When I get done with a book, I need a wind down time. Formatting the book allows me to get some of that out while still working. I enjoy it (for the most part … until Word decides it doesn't want to do something I keep telling it, it has to do.) It's an outlet for me. Something that challenges me. Again, it's my personal preference.

I think the world of Cassy and highly recommend her to you, if you're looking for a formatter, cover designer, or photog.

I made my decision for me. It gave me that time out after a book to pull my head out of my ass and get back in the game.

You need to decide if your time is better spent writing or doing the formatting yourself. You need to decide if you're ready to take the good with the bad when it comes to formatting and have the patience to hang in there when shit doesn't go right.

YouTube is your best fucking friend, people!!! You can learn anything on YouTube. No, I didn't say YouPorn, but you can learn a bunch of shit on there, too. Utilize the internet, people.

Chelsea's Chat:

I'M gonna keep this shit simple. Do you have the patience to try, fail, and try again? If not, pay a quality formatter.

I have done my own formats in Word. When I first started, it was a nightmare. The Zon likes page breaks, and Nook likes section breaks … It was all making me need a break.

When the time comes to upload, if you don't have an Apple computer, you won't be able to upload to iBooks direct, so you will have to use a distributor such as Smashwords or Draft2Digital. Uploading is a whole different can of worms as far as which sites to use and which ones require epubs versus docs, etc. We aren't covering those nitty gritty details. Maybe in the future, but this book is to motivate, not overwhelm you with the details.

Before I got my MacBook and could use Vellum, I used *IndieVention Designs* for my formatting. She added the graphics to my ebooks and paperbacks.

** I want to make a special note for you about graphics in ebooks. If your formatter doesn't embed the graphics properly, or you if you do your own, it will change your distribution cost in the Zon. This is a detail, but it's one that can be costly if you don't watch it.

If you aren't willing to go back and fix your shit and give yourself a learning curve on whatever formatting software you choose to use, then be willing to spend the cake for a formatter who will make your shit work right.

It's tedious. It's time consuming to a degree until you master it. Do not let this deter you. Set reasonable expectations.

There is a different format to ebooks than your paperbacks.

There are also different rules to paperbacks. You must set margins to fit your size. This is best done with the templates if you are doing your own. Please pay attention to every page because changing something on page 20 after you made it page 100 changes the following 80 pages after page 20. Every change effects everything that follows. I have rules for my paperbacks about spacing, where chapters start, etc., so it is important that, if you don't do the work yourself, you have a solid relationship with your formatter to get the final product you are looking for.

I'll keep it real. Whether I format on my own or use a formatter, I decide by my mood. Yes, it's a mood thing. Seriously, if I know I'm not in the mood to do my own, then I email my chick. Otherwise, I spend a day handling shit myself. It's not anything about her. It's about business. And I'll be frank:, if I sell a book for $0.99, I need to keep costs as low as possible to see a return on my investment. It costs cake to release a well-polished book.

Formatter Bullet Points

PAY UP OR SHUT UP! There are two options. Figure it out for yourself with grace, patience, and alcohol, or pay someone to do it for you.

CHAPTER SIX

MARKETING: IS NEVER ENDING!

L ook, this is crucial!

QUESTIONS TO ASK YOURSELF:

1. What is my budget?

2. What is my focus? Examples: reviews, sales, following, etc.

3. What is my plan? Handle my own or hire someone?

Chelsea's Chat:

OKAY, this is going to be hard to swallow. Marketing is always changing, and it's always going to be your BIGGEST challenge. This is a fundamentals book, so we are only briefly going to touch on marketing.

Please note: if you are an aspiring author, stay tuned for *Indie Insider: Marketing,* where we discuss branding and marketing yourself before you even finish writing the book. Now, if you're like Ryan and myself, you may already be published but struggling with marketing. No worries. *Indie Insider: Marketing* will help you as well. Just please know down to your core that the biggest challenge in the beginning is marketing. The biggest challenge in keeping your backlist alive as an established author is marketing.

Yes, I said biggest. Writing, editing, covers, that's all easy compared to figuring out what marketing works for you.

Honestly, Ryan and I could write an entire epic-length novel (100K words plus) on marketing failures. Yes, I said failures. We have spent years trying all sorts of things. We have spent countless hours comparing our strategies.

Guess what we came up with? There is no right answer and no simple way to make this work.

Marketing actually starts before you finish your book. But to go with the simplified version this book is intended to be … When it comes to a project, ask yourself what your marketing budget is, what's your focus, and what's the plan? Get your budget, your plan, and execute. If it doesn't work, then try something else. There is no promise about a damn thing in this business, except it takes drive and dedication.

Ryan's Ramblings:

LET'S GET REAL. This entire section will go on and on and on if we let it. There is so much here in this one little word *"marketing"* it makes me want to yack. Why? Because there is no magic butterfly that is going to sprinkle your shit and make it happen. Marketing is hard work. Really, really hard work.

You think typing *"the end"*, editing, and then sending your book off to a formatter means you're done?

Back it up! No, your journey has just begun. Actually, the marketing of a book should have started before this point. Since this is an overview and not an in depth nitty gritty, I'm going to try to contain myself. Please let us know if this is something you want in depth by emailing us.

Let's say, for overview purposes, you've written your book and it's at the editor, getting all shiny and pretty. What do you do at this point?

Hopefully, during your writing process, you already found your cover and have it good to go. If you don't, you'll want to do that ASAP!

First, choose a release date. Most of the time, you'll have this already done, but bear with me. Once you have that date, the fun begins! (Yes, I'm being a bit sarcastic. If you haven't figured out yet, I have that streak in me. You may want to go through and reread. lol.)

You need to decide if you want to hire a tour company to do your cover reveal, release day blitz, and book tour. I have worked with Ena from *Enticing Book Journey* for years. She's super sweet, knows her shit, and is fast as all hell. Her prices are very reasonable. I mean, like, very.

I've also worked with Lisa from the *Rockstars of Romance*. She's very professional and will help you at every turn you need.

There are quite a few other companies out there, as well. Do your homework!

On the flip side, you don't have to hire someone. You can do them yourself, BUT you need to have a very strong blogger list to do this. There is so much more to this, like, offer bloggers to sign up and don't spam them a billion times to share your book.

Moving on.

Once you have all those things set on your calendar, you start planning. The whole point of this is to build up excitement for your book. You do this with teasers, giveaways, book trailers, fun activities or games, FB posts, Twitter posts—everything on social media—and you get your reader group pumped up about the new book.

For me, I have a reader group, and I have a launch team. My reader group gets fun excerpts, my kooky thoughts while writing, pictures of my muse, and a shit ton of extras. My launch team gets all of that, plus they get the book early to review. My launch team kicks ass, and it's been a huge process in getting this team together. I'm still working out the kinks, but so far, it's been fantastic! The step by step of this is pretty lengthy, so my first suggestion is to build your reader group because that's where you'll find your launch team.

Getting all of these people pumped up for your book is important.

While my book is at the editor, I'm doing all of these things on hyper-drive. I'm making my own teasers, talking to my PA about daily and weekly ideas to get the excitement built up about the book—for me, this is my planning time. I have a book to get out into the world and *BAM!* I've got shit to do.

I do a ton of giveaways during the cover reveal, the week before release, release day, and release week. I mean A LOT. But, I budget for them! That's the key here. You need to make sure you keep within your budget. The best way to do this is to look at your previous book and see how much you made after expenses. This means EVERYTHING you put out into that book. See how much you can afford to spend on the newest one.

Yes, you hope that you'll make more cash on this one, but you need to be realistic. You don't want to spend hundreds or thousands of dollars on marketing when your last book put in two hundred bucks and didn't make a profit at the end. Be smart.

Here's something you need to keep in mind, as well. You'll fail. Yep. Sorry, Charlie, but you will. I have failed on so many occasions it's not even funny. I've lost money on so many things that it's laughable. Or, more like, cryable (my editor is going to be pissed at my made-up words).

Oh, just thinking of the money lost makes me want to break down …

Anywho.

The biggest thing with marketing is to get the energy going around your book. You want your readers to *have to* read your book. They are so pumped about it they are going to preorder it or buy it on release day.

Side note: I have so much to say about release day shit. Unfortunately, the thing as an author, a lot of it you'll spend on the Zon checking out your sales and your rank. I know … you just will. There will be that little voice in your head that says, *go do it!* Don't let the numbers or lack thereof get you down. Rankings now are so skewed it's not funny. Since the Zon came out with KU, the ranks aren't what they used to be. If you have a preorder, those ranks are even worse because you've already—according to the Zon—have been counted that sale. They don't dump them on release day and give you balloons and glitter then toss it in the air.

That's something you need to keep in mind.

There are authors who are ranking in the hundreds and still making lists for that week because they've sold so many. So please take the Zon rankings with a grain of salt.

This overview shit is hard! My little fingers want to keep typing like crazy, but these are the main marketing things.

Marketing Bullet Points

COVER REVEAL.

Release Blast.

Book Release Tour.

Sharing teasers, etc. to build up the excitement of your book. (Personally, I suggest you start this way early.)

Be active and available on release day. (If you have someone share your release, freaking tell them thank you!)

Know your budget! Don't go over it. It's soooooo easy to, but stick with it.

If something works for this release that blows it out of the water, you repeat it next time. If something fails, you chuck it and find something new. And just because something works for one doesn't mean it will work for you and vice versa.

CHAPTER SEVEN

SIGNINGS: I'M GONNA MAKE CAKE!

O h, the double-edged sword this one brings.

QUESTIONS TO ASK YOURSELF:
1. Can I overcome my own insecurities?
2. Is this a realistic time in my schedule?

Ryan's Ramblings:

THE INVITE COMES over your email about a signing you've been wanting to do forever. You immediately hit the *fuck yeah, I'm comin'* button. You're super stoked about going. Excited about the other authors attending and the money you're going to be bringing in, because it'll be a shit ton!

Let's slam on the brakes for a second. (Did ya feel your head jerk from my abruptness? Yes? Good.)

First off, signings are for two specific reasons.

One: To come face to face with your readers, give them your undivided attention, and to help your reader tribe become stronger.

Two: To interact and meet other authors.

Did you notice I said zero about making money in those two? If you're going for any other reason but these two, don't. Stay home.

Let's start with number one. Going to a signing is a fantastic way to give your readers one on one time with you. To get to know them as people and not just their Facebook pictures. Because, let's face it, some people we have to see their *picture* before connecting the dots.

Readers want to know you're human and not some robot behind a screen, pumping out words. They want to know that you are kind, nice, and attentive. You can show all of these things to your reader when you meet them face to face.

Well, Ryan, I'm super shy, and I don't "people" well. Totally get that. I don't *"people"* well, either. It doesn't mean you're a bad person. It just means you like to keep to yourself, have been burned in the past, or it's just your personality. None of this is wrong. It is something that you need to work on overcoming. Is it easy? Fuck no. But nothing in life worth having is. So, suck it up, buttercup.

If you plan on setting up your table all pretty-like and having the readers flock to your table when they have no clue who you are, you're missing the mark when it comes to signings. Like, by a hundred miles. Why? Because you're there to interact. That means getting up off your ass and doing so.

Example: I was in Cleveland last year (those women put on a kickass signing, by the way.) My table was two down from River Savage, who had a line out the ass. She's signing, smiling, and doing her thing. I had no one at my table. What did I do, even though it took a shit ton of digging deep? I got off my ass, grabbed some of my bookmarks, and infiltrated her line. Yep, I sure as hell did. I had a free book that everyone just has to read, of course!

I wasn't a douche about this, and if someone didn't want to talk to me, I'd smile and move on. But the point is: I was on the move. I didn't wait for those readers to come to me. I didn't sit there and hope, *if I only had a few more readers like XYZ had*. Nope, I got off my ass and got to work.

Another example: Nashville. Another kickass event! The entirety of the signing, I sat maybe twenty to thirty minutes. That means I was on my feet for five or six hours straight. Did my feet, legs, and back hurt? Fuck yeah. Did I have an absolute blast? Hell yes! Anyone who came near my table, I introduced myself, told them what kind of books I write, and offered them a free book. Yep! *Ravage Me* is free on all channels. I use that shit. Why? Because everyone likes free, myself included. If you can hook a reader in by letting them see what you can do with your words with one book, you've got a new reader, and therefore, have added a new person to your reader tribe.

The bottom line is: get off your ass and mingle. If your line is to the door, of course you're not going to get up and mingle. Be smart about it.

What happens over time is you find your core people, the readers who go to several signings a year and you repeatedly see their faces. You get to know them. Know what they do for a living, and many tell you about their children. There's something with them that you can relate to and that builds the connection between the two of you. That connection over more time gets stronger. The whole point of it is to BUILD RELATIONSHIPS.

Now, Ryan, I only have one book out there and no one knows I exist.

Trust me; someone knows you exist. It could be your mom coming to the signing to show you support. Your husband or friend. Someone knows you exist. That is your building platform. While at the singing, you draw in their strength and do your introductions to new readers, offer them swag, and be a genuine person with them.

My first signing, I was scared shitless. Not gonna sugarcoat it one bit. It was in Orange Beach, Alabama, and I had four books out, I believe. Nervous was my full name, not my middle. My husband thought for sure I'd bounce away with how fast my leg moved up and down. I didn't know why the hell I was there. Why would anyone want to see little old me from Podunk, Illinois?

But I went, with my chin up and ready to roll. Had my table set up all pretty-like, swag out for people to nab, and books ready to go. As the moments ticked by before the signing started, I convinced myself that no one would come to my table. That me being there was a total waste.

Then something happened I'll never forget. Amber (she was either a helper at the signing or with another author—I can't remember which) came up to my table and grabbed a couple of bracelets off my table. She said, "You've got a reader outside with your shirt on. I'm gonna go give them these." For that moment in time, everything stopped. I had readers outside with my shirt on? *Holy fucking shit!*

The smile on my face was broad and the leg twitch only got faster because … *I had a reader!* Yep, total dork but don't give a shit. When it was time to open the door, sure enough, the reader and her friend, who had my shirt on, too, came directly to my table. I was on cloud nine. Nervous as all hell, but I pushed it aside and greeted my readers.

Now, four years later, that reader, Kimberly, is now one of my trusted beta readers. We chat regularly. She's not only in my tribe, she's in my fold. If I wouldn't have taken my ass to that signing, had all those insecure thoughts, I wouldn't have met Kimberly. I wouldn't have that connection with someone who lives hundred miles away from me. It made every single moment of that trip worth it.

Two: Meeting new authors. This is NOT ass kissing 101, people. You like the taste of shit, this part isn't for you. There is a difference between being genuine with meeting someone and kissing their ass. We're all people. All colleagues. We're also all on different levels. It is what it is. Again, suck it up.

When you go to signings, don't go in with the intent that you're going to go to every single table and make sure that your name is known! That's shit. Also, don't go into it with the "*I'm gonna make her/him my new best friend.*" No, no, and no. Relationships don't work that way, and since you're reading this and write fictional romance, you should know this.

No one is going to be your friend in one day. No one is going to see you and think you are truthful and trustworthy. It just won't happen. Why? Because many of us have been burned in one way or the other over time. Many of us have had relationships that ended up going south and combusted on the ground. We're cautious about who we let into our circle. It isn't that we are bitches. There are some out there, of course, because the world wouldn't go around if there weren't. It's that our insides have been shredded more than once and we are protecting ourselves from that.

If you are a very outgoing person, walking up to an author is easy for you. More power to ya. Introduce yourself. If you have a book of theirs you like/love, tell them. All authors love to hear that. But don't be fake. If you haven't read their shit, don't say you have.

I've been tempted a couple of times to ask a fellow author a question about my book when they just loved it but didn't name the main characters off of said book. I didn't, but that is not a genuine connection. That is someone who wants something from you. Those are the people you don't need in your life.

There have been three instances that I can recall offhand that have rocked me when meeting authors. One was Kristen Ashley, because *HELLO!!!* it's KA! She's super sweet and the smile on her face never leaves. I've read almost all of her shit and am a huge fangirl.

My visit to her wasn't professional in the typical sense. I wasn't there to suck her ass, become her new BFF, or ride her coattails in the wind. No, my purpose was to tell her how much I loved Eddie and Luke, plain and simple. Oh, and to get those two books signed from her. It wasn't to schmooze her or get anything from her. No, it was true, honest, and she gave me her time, putting me on cloud nine.

Second was T.M. Frazier. Now, I sat with her the year prior at a table at Wicked Book Weekend, but was scared shitless to talk to her. I didn't have the skin I have now, so my best tactic was avoidance. Which was stupid, stupid, stupid! But live and learn. The next year, I had to meet her because she gave the world King, Preppy and Bear. To say I was nervous was an understatement.

Terri Anne (Browning) was there with me, and I convinced her (okay, she says that I pulled her and said she's coming with me—whichever) to walk up to T.M.'s table with me.

My body started shaking. Yep, shaking. When I handed her my books, my hands had tremors. This isn't because she's not nice as all hell. No, it's because I'm a total fangirl. And a nut, but that's another story.

T.M. was super nice and put up with all my shit, while all I could think about was that first meeting I had with her, sitting at a table, and too scared to say anything to her. If I would have introduced myself, broken the ice, I think my second experience wouldn't have been so nerve racking. Live and learn. LEARN being the key word here.

Third was meeting Jenkia Snow. Eep! Love her books! And when I learned she was shy, too, all that melted away.

Did you notice with my three examples there wasn't one word of what those authors could do for me? There wasn't a *"if I become friends with her, I can tap into their reader bases, blah, blah, blah."* No, not a word on that. Why? Because that's not honest or genuine. You don't form and build relationships with people for that reason.

When you meet authors at signings, if you're not doing it from a place that's good and not self-serving inside yourself, don't bother. People can see through this shit. They'll scream *FAKE* at you all day long. No one wants to entrust themselves, their work, or their career/name on someone who is fake and unworthy. We all work damn hard to get where we are, and that's why circles are small. You have to earn your spot in my circle. I'm not saying that to be a bitch. I'm being real. Because once you're in, you're in. I'm loyal to the core. But it takes a bit to get it.

Now, those authors above, are they in my core authors? Nope. Would it be kickass if they were? Yep. Am I going to dwell and be upset that they aren't? Nope. Why? Because I met those authors for me. For me to express to them what I liked about their work. It was honest and pure.

That doesn't mean that I'd push myself on any of them. Not gonna happen. If one were to message me and start of up a conversation, hell yeah, I would reciprocate. But I'm not going to PM all of my new release information a thousand times a day, begging for them to share my work. Why? Because that's an ass move. That relationship isn't there. I don't know if they've ever read me, so why would I want someone to pimp me that doesn't know my work?

I'm pretty sure I totally side-tracked on this entire section, but it is what it is.

Oh, money! See what I mean? Forgot.

We need to chat about all that cake you're gonna be bringing home after a signing. Let's talk expenses first.

Now, depending on where you are, you'll need to figure out transportation. For me, if it's far, I fly because being in a car that long isn't for me. If it's close, I'll drive, but up until recently, I didn't have a new car. So, if I did this, I needed to rent a car.

Let's do round numbers; it makes life easier. I'll pretend that I'm driving to a signing instead of flying. Pretty much add $1000 to the end of this and you'll get the full effect of that option, as well.

Car: $500 (It's actually more, but I'm going round, people.)

Gas: $150

Hotel: $500

Createspace: $300 (You gotta have books to sell.)

Swag: $200

Table Fees: $250

Food: $150

Clothes, shoes, miscellaneous: $150

This comes out to $2200

Now, if you sell your books for $14 a pop, you need to sell one hundred and fifty books to BREAK EVEN. Yes, you heard me. One hundred and fifty books just to break even. Now, you sell that many books, more power to ya! But the reality is, most of us aren't. If you go into it thinking you are, you'll come out on the other end thinking it was a shit signing. When in fact, it wasn't. You just didn't have your goals and objectives met. That's on you. You need to change your thoughts on these.

Now, are there some authors who make a hell of a profit? Of course! That's wonderful, but not everyone is going to have that outcome, and if you're pushing that thought, you'll be setting yourself up for failure. Which none of us need.

Side note: The Alabama signing was the first one where I met Chelsea Camaron. Yeah, she scared the living shit out of me, but I said hi and went on my way. *HA!!!* And look at us now. A series together, crossovers together, and now this. It just proves that if you don't put yourself out there, you won't know what the future will hold.

Chelsea's Chat:

WELL, Ryan Michele totally nailed my thoughts on events and where they "fit" in your career.

Let me tell you about that Alabama event where Ryan and I met …

It was small. Yeah, not rocking and rolling, but I am good with that. Ryan Michele approached me, a Michelle beside her (sorry, Michelle, I forgot your last name. It's not you. I promise it's me. I suck with names).

I was getting ready to leave, and she said, "Oh, hi, you're Chelsea Camaron. I'm Ryan Michele."

I said, "Awesome. What do you write?"

She replied, "*Ravage MC*."

I freaked the fuck out. Not because I read her books. No, I hadn't. But you know what? I remembered those two women with those *Ravage Me* T-shirts. Kimberly Roe and her friend wore these *Ravage* shirts, and alongside them was the Jessica Hamm. Jessica is the funniest and nicest person I have ever met. I love Kim, too, and we share dessert every event together now—it's our thing. ;) I remember going on and on, obnoxiously so, to Ryan Michele about her girls and their T-shirts.

Real deal? I was in total fangirl mode over Ryan Michele's fangirls. I mean, they had *Ravage Me* T-shirts!!! I thought that was the coolest thing ever. Still do. And somehow, even after all this time, I don't have one of these shirts … I think I need to fix this.

Alas, that meeting was great. We connected. We went home, and I think Ryan sent me a Facebook friend request right after, or maybe it was before. You should know that I fucking hate social media.

No, no, let me rephrase. I'm allergic to the word *social*. It makes me get hives and itchy. Yes, signings are social, and I'm awkward as fuck for the first hour. I get all in my head about them. It's way out of my comfort zone, but it's necessary.

Yup, I said it. *Necessary*.

Look, the Indie industry is not like traditional publishing. You don't get a marketing team. And let me be clear that there are quite a few traditional publishers who will still leave marketing in your hands. Read your contract. But, this is later discussed in marketing. In the Indie community, you need to network.

Everyone has a different experience. You can learn from them all.

So, events ... yeah, you need to do them occasionally, and you need to get over yourself. It's about the experience. Whether no one knows you or not, you need to put yourself out there. If you were brave enough to release your book baby into the world, stand behind your work and show it off, and not in an arrogant way, but professionally.

Networking is not about what someone can do for you. It is about sharing experiences and learning together. Do NOT think another author owes you a damn thing. They don't.

Look, I don't know how many times I've heard or seen on social media lately, *"Oh, get a big author to pimp your book."*

Hold on tight. I'm gonna get real.

Coattails are something tailors sew and fix. Authors don't.

If you're an ass kisser, stop reading. If you think someone else will make your career, stop reading. Grab a mirror and go find yourself.

This business is one where you have to be yourself, own yourself, and make it for yourself. It's not about getting rich. If you think that, stop reading.

My first year, I was in the negative. My husband paid for all my book shit out of his income. I was a stay-at-home mom, struggling with my identity. I didn't want to just be his wife. I'm a badass all on my own. As much as I kept writing and kept losing money, he stood behind me.

I'm talking thousands of dollars here, people, and he let me blow it, not knowing if I would ever have a real return on his investment. And the man is a businessman. His job was business and bottom lines, no joke.

My first event was in Georgia, spring of 2014. My husband paid my way because my books were just starting to break even. I went and excitedly met Katie Ashley. I may have teared up when she came to my table and told me she read *One Ride* and wanted to buy a signed copy. I met S.M. Donaldson at this event, too. She actually was the first person to approach me, and I told her she was looking for someone else. She set me straight that, no, it was me, and when was *Forever Ride* coming out because she needed answers on Tank. Well, years later, she is one of my closest friends and biggest supporters on the days I want to quit.

I went to that event with very little. I didn't want to take money from my husband and kids when I wasn't really sure this was going to pan out.

I left with a whole new outlook on my career.

I didn't make a profit.

Events cost money to attend. Do not set yourself up to think you will make money at an event. Go for the experience. Go and enjoy time with likeminded people. Go and meet readers who are as passionate about the written word as you are.

Jessica Hamm, Kim Tatum, Leah Michele, Dawn LoPresti, and so many other readers absolutely amaze me at events. They sit down with me, and I swear they can tell you more about my books than I can.

In July, 2014, I was attending an event in North Carolina, my home state. At the time, we lived in Louisiana, so I was happy to have an excuse to be home. I met a reader named Pam and her husband Boomer. They are an amazing couple. The way they are together, the love in Boomer's eyes with every look he gave Pam … it's the shit we write romance books about.

I wrote a book about them. Truth. I wrote them into my series. If I hadn't met Boomer at that event, the *Hellions Ride* series would be very different and have one less book in it today. My life would not be brightened with their spirits and the random texts I send Pam because she simply makes me smile.

Go to events, not to make money, but to feed your talents and be around people who know what it is to listen to the voices inside their heads, too.

To be clear, though, signings take preparation. A lot behind the scenes goes into attending an event. Books need to be ordered, swag, and your travel plans set. The week of the event, you will have little time to write, because you will need to prep your preorders, organize your swag, your banner, your everything. Then, traveling is a day there and a day home typically, and the day of the event. Therefore, you have three days solely focused on the event itself, even after your prep. When you come home, you have a day to unwind, sort through the blogger business cards, author business cards, and other items you obtained. You have to unpack your books, swag, etc., and sort out what you sold out of and need more of.

There is at least one solid day after just getting your shit unsorted that you sorted for the event.

If you can't keep up with your writing, work, life, and events, then make sure you don't overbook yourself because these things are time-consuming. Don't schedule an event when you know you have a deadline, unless you really can work from a hotel. I can't concentrate, so most events I don't even bother taking my laptop anymore.

Figure out what works for you, even if it's one event a year. And go in with eyes wide open in your expectations.

Signing Bullet Points

DON'T EXPECT to make cake!
Step outside of your comfort zone!
Talk to everyone!

CHAPTER EIGHT

NEXT: YES, THERE NEEDS TO BE A NEXT!

T here is only one question here, I suppose …
What do I do next?

Ryan's Ramblings:

RYAN, I wrote a book, put it out, did all the marketing stuff, and it's just there. Sales are slow. Crawling. What do I do?

This one's gonna sting.

Ready?

Write the next book. *Bam!*

I know what you're thinking. *But, I put so much time into this book and it didn't do anything. I did everything I thought I should do and it just sat there. I need to make money off this book.*

Reality time. That book, at that point, is done. An author is going to make most of their sales on preorders and that first week the book is out. It's just the fact.

Does it hurt? Fuck yeah! When I put out *Needing to Fall*, in my head, I thought, *this is it. This book is gonna be that "everyone wants to read it" book.* I pimped it. I gave it to whoever would read that sucker. I did the teasers, trailer, ran FB ads. I had my tours set up and reviewers lined up. As many tears as I shed writing that book, I just knew it would take. I knew it, dammit!

The cover was beautiful and a perfect depiction of my story. And I say *my story* because there is a shit ton of myself in that book. You really want to know me? Want to know what the rabbit hole is about? There's the book you need to read. Sidetracked. Sorry.

When this book released, I had four hundred and twenty-seven preorders. That book has only sold 3K copies total. It's been out for over a year. Over a year, people! The book I thought would be "the one" didn't become what I wanted it to be.

Do I love that book? Fuck yes. Did I need to write it? Yes. You notice there I asked NEED to write it? Yes, I was in a dark place at that time and it was the only way to get those demons out. For me, it was my release from them. Career-wise, it didn't do what I wanted it to do.

I've made back the money I put into it … barely. But that's as far as it goes. I haven't actually made money on that book.

I know, I'm veering. The point is, after that book, I wrote the next. Then I wrote the next. And I wrote the next. You have to have thick skin, ladies and gents. These hits are going to come. Some of the most famous authors didn't have their books be a hit right away. Some even had their books out for-freaking-ever before someone discovered them. Or, their first book didn't hit, but that fourth one they put out did. That's part of this world. There are zero guarantees.

That being said, you write the next book. You did everything you could for that book before. Now, you need to focus your time on the next book. You need to put aside all of those hurt feelings (if you have them) or happy feelings (if your book kicked ass, but that defeats the purpose of this), and you write the next damn book.

That being said, don't totally forget about that book like it doesn't exist. You still share it on your FB, have your reader group pimp it, etc. But your focus needs to be on writing that next book.

Your backlist of books is what is going to sustain you. Please reread that sentence. It's an important one. One I probably should bold, highlight, and cap. Your backlist of books is what is going to sustain you in having a successful career.

How can you say that? Because that's where I make my money each month. My backlist of books that sit there on the Zon, iBooks, Google Play, Nook, and Kobo, ready and waiting for someone to come along and buy them.

Now, think about it … There are millions and millions of readers out there. You have three out of that million pick up one of your books. You have ten pick another and buy it. Then you have twenty-five others who find different books of yours. Then, say you have some in Kindle Unlimited, which is a whole different Indie Insider book, let me tell you, and you get 3K pages read that day. Let's add this up.

You have 38 books that people have bought at $3.99 a pop, leaving you with $2.65 (we'll take out delivery because the Zon gets their $$) That leaves you making $100 (rounded). Add in about $15 (it's .004x pages read for KU) for your KU books, and you're at $115.

$115 for 30 days is $3400 a month. This is all rounded numbers, so you can see where I'm coming from.

But this is without a release that month. This is just from your backlist. See how having a large one can help you build your income? Now, I have twenty-six books on my back list. That's quite a few. Having one or two on your backlist won't do this for you.

But, if you keep pushing on, writing that next book, building your brand, expanding your reader tribe, making genuine connections with other authors, set your marketing up to par, you can get there.

If you're saying $3400 isn't enough for you, then you may need to think of something else, like a second job. Or a main job and writing is your "second" job. Yep, I said it. Because there will be months when you make $500, which means selling a total of about one hundred and eighty books that month. That's just the way the market is. If you are counting on this money to sustain you, you need to take that focus elsewhere. It will not help your books. It will only bring the tone of them down to where you're dipping low from the last book not making it.

Would it be a perfect world if we each made that 3K every single month like clockwork and could depend on it? Fuck yes. But it's not reality, and you need to take care of your family. Selling thirty-eight books a day to make the income listed above could be a goal you strive for.

Readers are smart. So damn smart. They pick up on when you're down. They pick up on a lot.

I think I've strayed away again. *CC!!!!* She really needs to put a leash on me.

My best advice is for you to sit down and write the next book and build up your backlist.

Chelsea's Chat:

CC, where are the questions? I mean, all these points, you have questions to ask myself. Yeah, sorry, folks, when it comes to what's next, well, it's the next book. That's it.

Writing is a process. Once you go from concept to the end and release that bad boy into the world ... that book is done. You have to move on.

Yes, there are authors who go *BOOM* on only one book or series, but reality bites, and it isn't commonplace.

Backlist is my favorite word. "Next" is my other favorite word, right up there with fuck. Okay, well, I'm sure you're rolling your eyes, thinking, *"Hey, broad, you have a crazy long backlist; it's easy for you to say."*

Yup, it sure as shit is.

Look, I get asked lots from first-time authors what to do, and my answer is always the same: keep writing.

Yes, on to the next work. Period. It's not rocket science, people. You have your plan, you work it, and when the book is out, it's out. You can't change what the sales will be if you've followed your plan.

Now, if you fail to follow your plan, you failed, so your sales are on your lack of execution.

Notice there are a lot of yous in that sentence.

Welcome to Indie life. Your shit is on you. If something isn't working, it's up to you to own that shit and change it. There is nobody to blame, and no one to fix shit.

My mindset is like playing chess. When my release is out to the world, I am already in works on my next release. The moment my book is uploaded, I switch gears. I go to my marketing peeps, finalize what needs to be handled for release preparation, and then immediately move on.

I can't stress enough that this is a business. If someone says it's a hobby, they're right for them. It probably is a hobby, and they aren't concerned with making money. They also are probably struggling with what really to do next.

Don't get offended. Get real with yourself.

This is a business. The Zon makes shit tons of cake off Indie authors. And guess what? You can make your own chunk of the change consistently, but you can't do it treating it like a hobby.

Shit stings, but it's real.

This is a business, so treat it so.

I could write a whole book on making this a real career and how to really put in the hours and drive like a regular job. I'm not going to do that here.

I'm simply going to say: write the next book, and then the next, and keep going.

WHERE ARE THE BULLET POINTS?
Write the next book … simple.

CHAPTER NINE

SCHEDULES: BALANCE IS NON-EXISTENT, OR IS IT?

O kay, don't get all twisted. You must decide: is this part-time or full-time?

We can't make that decision for you, but you have to decide.

Look, if part-time is all you can do, then it's all you can do, but schedule appropriately.

Questions to ask yourself:

1. How much time to I have to dedicate to my writing?

2. What is the best use of the time I have?

3. Are my goals realistic?

Chelsea's Chat:

SOME OF YOU may get upset with what I'm about to tell you. I apologize if that's the case, but I never promised to sugarcoat shit, kay?

If this is full-time, then sweetheart, you damn well better treat it full-time. That means, shut the social media off, cut your TV off, your phone—it's all gone and you treat this like a job where you have to stand and work for at least eight hours a day.

I'm a hardass. In fact, the first time Ryan approached me about even reading a book for a simple opinion, I replied with: *you need to know I'm a hardass.*

Honestly, real deal, I should come with a warning: *Sweetest bitch you'll ever know. I give my heart to the peeps in my inner circle, but I also hold nothing back. What you see is what you get.*

I'm extremely driven. In fact, it's what has gotten me this far in this business. And anyone who wants to be in my inner circle knows if you don't have the drive in your life, I'm going to make you crazy with mine. I push myself to the limit and beyond.

If you can't push yourself, then you really are going to struggle in the Indie world.

I can't make your schedule for you.

I can tell you that I suffer from an auto-immune disease that can sometimes be completely debilitating, but I still work. EVERY

DAY. Yes, I said it. My family will tell you, my friends will tell you, no matter how sick, I do something for my career every day.

You decide what you can give to this time-wise, and you make a schedule. And dammit, you stick to it as much as possible.

It's easy in this industry to say, *"I'll do it tomorrow, or next week, or I'll make up the word count later."* Days slip away, and then months. Then you become irrelevant, your work not known like before, unseen … and then you have to start all over.

Even on the bad days, some words written or a task completed is better than nothing. Push through and make shit happen. NO ONE WILL MAKE IT HAPPEN FOR YOU. Make it for yourself!

Ryan's Ramblings:

I VERY MUCH DISLIKE SCHEDULES. I need them. They're important. But, adhering to them sucks sometimes. This can mean your daily schedules, yearly book schedules … hell, life schedules—all of them.

I'm going to try to break this down so I'm no scattered all over the damn place because, let's be frank, I tend to do that.

Daily schedules. Do I have a set schedule such as, "I will spend one hour on FB, two hours returning emails, etc.?" No. I work pretty much all the time. If I'm not on my laptop, I'm on my phone, which I'm still trying to learn to be able to copy and paste shit to make my life easier. If I'm not writing, I'm doing the paperwork, answering emails, answering PMs on FB, checking sales, writing blog posts, updating my website, making teaser graphics, organizing the next books tour, talking with other author friends, chatting with Chelsea about these ideas that pop into our heads and we're ready to scream.

I don't have much downtime, which is something that I plan on changing this year. Yes, I'm seriously driven. One can't say they want to put out a book a month, and then sit back with their finger up their ass. It doesn't work that way, people.

You want something, you work for it. No fairy is going to come down from the sky and plop your income in your lap.

I've always worked hard. As a teacher, I worked all the damn time, trying to make shit right for my kids. As an author, it's not different, except I work harder. Yep, you heard me. I'm up until all hours of the night doing something. I can't tell you the last time I watched television that wasn't just playing in the background. (Side note: listening to SpongeBob's laugh while writing a sex scene totally kills the mood.)

I used to have a to-do list. I fucking loved that thing. I could cross shit off and feel like I accomplished so much in one day, when it didn't feel like I did squat. Writing this is reminding me I need to get back to doing that. I lost it somewhere along the last three months, and I need to find it again.

This is what I did.

I bought me one of those fancy calendars that has the month and the days laid out. I went in and put all the big stuff on the month—signings, releases (that I know about), anniversaries of books releases, and birthdays, because I can't remember shit. What I did every morning after getting my kids on the school bus was sit down with my calendar and on that day, write a to-do list. When I first started, I'd only write three to five things. Some of those were small, like take a shower, for example.

After I accomplished whatever goal that was, I'd cross it off and put some goofy-ass smiley face thing. It was an ACCOMPLISHMENT for the day and needed something. Hell, there were times when I'd do the dishes, then go to my to-do list, add that fucker on there, and cross it off, just so I could visually see that I did something that day. Some days are damn hard, but those helped me.

And now, I'm going to start doing them again that I'm writing this, so thanks for that! It's amazing how we forget shit until it smacks us in the face.

A big thing with "schedules" is to know the best time of the day for you to write. Mine is the late afternoon/night. This sucks royally because it's the time when my kids come home from school, homework, dinner, baths, etc.

This really doesn't come as a surprise to me because I've always been a night owl. Even teaching, I had to be hooked up to a Diet Coke IV to get moving. By the afternoon, I was ready to kickass.

Once you know the best time your brain works to write, work around that. You're not going to want to do the paperwork stuff during your peak writing time. You're going to want to get words down.

But, Ryan, didn't you just say you had tons of shit going on at that time? How do you do it?

My kids love to play outside. After homework, outside they go. I may only have an hour, but I can lay some serious words down in an hour. I make dinner, we eat, talk—all that parent stuff. Kids like their downtime in their room. *Bam!* There's another hour for me to get in words. We do baths, bed, books, etc., and after that last goodnight, I have a good three hours to nail out words.

My husband is gone a lot for work, but when he's home, I alter things so I can spend time with him, too. It may mean that I stay up an hour later to finish whatever thought I have rolling through my head, but it works.

You have to find what works for you. If you're a morning bird like CC, you can nail your shit out and not have to worry or think about it the rest of the day, so you choose. If you're like either of us, though, you'll be adding more words as the day goes on.

Did you know that, if you write two thousand words a day, you can have a full-length novel done in one month? Thirty days, people! Really think about that for a moment. In one month, you could have a book done.

Now, reality check time! That's not always going to happen because words some days don't want to flow and you want to toss your computer into a river. Still, if you write 1K words a day, you can get a book done in sixty days. Or 500 hundred words in ninety days.

Those words, you could decide they are shit words and need to be chucked.

Once, I deleted over 50K and had a meltdown. But, if you get the words down, you can work with them, adjust them. Maybe some of those words give you an idea that will blow your book out of the water.

NEVER DELETE. I know I just said above I deleted those 50K. Really, I moved them over to another doc that stated *"deleted scenes."* I didn't put 99% of those words back in the doc at the end, so I now consider them deleted, as heart breaking as that is.

Let's talk schedules for books. The good news is, you're an Indie author and your own boss. You don't like your schedule or don't like when you thought you'd put XYZ book out, you can change it. That being said, if you have a preorder on the Zon, you can't. Okay, technically, you can move it up, but you can't push it back. Rewind. You can, BUT you lose all your preorder privileges for a year. I know! Holy fuck! Therefore, you need to be really clear if you set up a preorder and have that shit nailed down. Or else, suffer the wrath of the Zon!

Schedules Bullet Points

THE MORE YOU WORK, the more you get out in your career. That being said, balance and don't leave your family flailing in the dust.

Use your time wisely. Time is money. Money is time.

CHAPTER TEN

AGENTS, DEALS, HYBRID: HOW TO DO IT ALL … OR NOT!

T his is a very personal decision. Having a publishing contract is not for everyone.

QUESTIONS TO ASK YOURSELF:
1. Why do I want to sign with an agent?
2. Why do I want to sign this deal?
3. Why do I want to seek out a deal?
4. Can I afford to sign this work away?
5. Is this work really meant to be traditionally published?

Chelsea's Chat:

I WANT to open this up by being very clear …

I am a hybrid author. My experience is my own, and everyone has a different experience. This is not the Bible on getting a book deal.

Okay. Agents, they have a tough job.

Before you ever query an agent, please understand that time is precious. They get hundreds to thousands of queries a day. If you are not willing to give up a portion of your royalties to your agent for the job they are going to provide, then don't ever start the process in the first place.

Agents don't work for FREE. They get a percentage of the royalties of each contract they negotiate on your behalf. Their job is to help you find the right fit for your manuscript and guide you through the process of getting signed. Their job is also to be very frank with you about your work, which means, if they don't see the marketing potential in mainstream, they won't pick it up. It's not you, it's not your work; it's a business.

Mainstream market is strong in character development; clear, precise plots; and not overly controversial.

Please note: this is for an unknown author trying to get signed on a debut.

The world is different if you have a following, because your agent, your publisher, and yes, even secondary rights, such as foreign rights and audio, will ask about your following on social media, as well as sales numbers from previously self-published work.

A publisher is going to be putting a lot of money and man hours into your manuscript. They need to know they can make a quick return on their investment. An agent goes through the queries, searching for the story that stands out and has the potential to be popular to a wide audience.

In the future, we may address writing styles and writing for mainstream readers, as well as niches to really specialize your style, but this book doesn't have enough space for me to go there. (Again, I'm a technical writer, so every word I write has a purpose in a bigger picture. Every book I've written, I analyzed in niche, marketability, and where it can crossover because I am not a mainstream author. I do write to my niche. There is a technical mentality in the way an agent or publisher's representative looks at your book, and I promise you it isn't merely your concept.)

So first, decide if you can handle giving up a cut of all future royalties on your work to your agent before you query.

Then, the dreaded search. Finding an agent isn't about sending a query to every agent you can find contact information on. No, you need to study their likes, dislikes, and whether they are even open to submissions. Most of this is found on their websites or social media profiles.

Write your query. Look, there are loads of books out there with tips for this. I won't overwhelm you here with how to write a query. I will say, if you don't like writing blurbs, then a query is worse than the deepest pits of Hell, okay? It isn't easy.

So, you got yourself an agent! What now?

Well, the agent will usually ask what you're looking for and give you a plan for what they think they can sell. Some books are not going to get paperback deals.

I know you want to kill me right now. I'm a dream chaser, too, but business is business and paperback deals aren't smart business for most publishers. They have to produce such large quantities, and then they sit on a shelf, collecting dust. That's not good business. If you were a publisher, you wouldn't want to waste money like that, either. So, don't get hung up on getting a paperback deal right away.

You also need to understand that rejection stings.

If you think having a publishing deal validates you in some way, think again. Please don't sign with an agent, and then with a publisher because you think it's an easy in or will get you to the top of the charts.

When you sign your work over, they control more than you realize ... until you are neck deep in it.

Look, I'm not knocking it. I will happily turn over work for my publisher any time they will accept it. Key words there: accept it.

I have four books with a traditional publisher, and guess what? I still get rejections. Seriously, it happens.

I could let it fester and fuck with my head, and there was a time I did. Then, I just finished that book and released it on my own. Actually, it was six books that were rejected, but hey, who's counting? (Well, I'm counting my money in the bank because I self-pubbed and still made a profit).

And I will still tell you that I love my editors and team with my publisher, even if they turn down more than they accept from me. It's a truly unique experience, and I have learned so much that I have carried over into my writing style.

Oh, yes, that word "style." See, you have to remember that publishers are in this for the big business, the mass market, which is used to a certain writing style. So, some of the things in a self-published book that gets passed by can't happen in their world, and it has made me a stronger writer.

Sure, it killed my ego, because I'm just not that good, and they fixed me to fit their world. But, my ego survived, and I grew.

The entire process with an agent and publisher is so different than doing it on your own. There are things I can't talk about because contracts—well, NDAs, people—but I can say that you need to know your contract and not trust your agent to give you all the information.

It's a lot to take in, and this is a personal decision, whether it's something for you or not.

I love being a hybrid author. I love the work I give to my publisher and broadening my skillsets. I love the freedom of my self-published titles because, even if they don't make me bucket loads of money, they are my stories, done my way.

I could go on and on about agents and publishers, and I am happy to help anyone in their journey, but I want this section to be clear that signing a deal doesn't make you a superstar. Simply going for your dreams makes you a superhero all on its own. This is a personal decision, and I support whichever way anyone chooses to go.

Ryan's Ramblings:

I KNOW shit on this topic. I'm Indie, through and through. I like it that way and don't plan on doing any queries for agents at this time. Now, if you're reading this down the road and I have, then I changed my mind. Best thing about being Indie is that I can change my damn mind!

I'll let Chelsea give you her wisdom here because I just don't have any. Peace. (I blame that on my eleven-year-old).

Agents Bullet Points

THIS IS a personal decision to query an agent or sign a publishing deal. Not having one does NOT define you, having one does not promise you a flourishing career. Take the pressure off and do your best work and let that work stand for itself both to an agent or to a reader if you choose to self-publish.

CHAPTER ELEVEN

LISTS, LISTS, LISTS: THEY CAN CUT A BITCH.

What doesn't kill us…

SOME THINGS TO ASK YOURSELF:

1. Why do I want to make a list?
2. What changes when I make a list?

This shit is going to get deep and some people may not like what we have to say, but again, these are our opinions, plain and simple.

Ryan's Ramblings:

WHAT ARE THE LISTS?

Okay, have you been in the author world for any amount of time? Do you watch your newsfeed on Facebook? Then you have to know what the LISTS are.

USA Today, *NYT* and the *Wall Street Journal* are your three biggies, the ones you will hope to reach at some point in your career and wish and pray on a star that you'll achieve. To get on these lists, you have to sell a shit ton of books. There are no ifs, ands, or buts about it.

Now, the number for each of them is different, and I haven't found a specific place on the internet that states the exact numbers. Let's just put it as this: you need to sell a shit ton. Like, at least over eight thousand copies in that first week, probably more.

This is a combination of all sites—Amazon, iTunes, Nook, Kobo, and Google Play. NOT through Draft2Digital or Smashwords, as they don't always update in the same timeframes! There are so many variables in achieving one of these lists that it's impossible for anyone to ever know if their name will show up. Even the big guys have to wait to see that list pop up because there are zero guarantees.

Me? I've never been on any of these lists. There was a point in my career, not too long ago, when making one of these lists started to consume me. Eat at me. Fester at me. I mean, shit, I've done this for four years now and it has been a goal for me from the beginning. Now, the problem I have is that I let it become more of an infestation. A must have to prove my worth. An *"everyone has it but me"* thing for quite a while. I'm not proud of that shit, but I'm sharing it so you get me. I was there, deep, thinking the whole *"what's wrong with me and my books?"* That answer is nothing, but let me continue.

Having this mentality sucked every bit of fun out of writing away for me. It put out my flame and kyboshed everything that used to burn inside of me when I began to write a book. I went down the rabbit hole. For those who don't know, the rabbit hole is a term CC and I use when we get down low. We all go there at some point. It's how you pick yourself up is what matters.

After this last time of feeling down in the dumps, I realized, like some magical puff of a unicorn, that I didn't want this anymore. I wanted to get back to my happy. I wanted to enjoy writing again and not feel like a loser because those lists weren't attached to my name. I wanted to feel the stories I wrote and not be some robot pumping things out just to see if something would take off. This is never a good idea; trust me. I learned that, NO, I'm not a loser because I haven't made a list, and neither are you. NEITHER ARE YOU!

So, I turned it around. How? I started looking at the positives instead of falling down the rabbit hole.

Let's take my latest release *Bound by Family*. Now, I wasn't going to write this book. I didn't want to, at all. I mean, would readers really want to read about the next generation of bikers? And more importantly, can I write a character now having sex and taking names that I wrote as a child? My readers pushed, and it was the best thing they ever did for me.

Why?

When I started that book, it flowed because I knew the history. I knew the family. I knew the type of man that would come out of his parents. I connected. I wrote. For once in a really long time, I wrote with a damn smile on my face. It ended up being a kickass book. Hands down, one of my best. It was my happy. That in and of itself was worth every minute working on it.

I didn't make a list with this book. Not gonna lie and say I didn't check the day the *USA* list came out. Sick or not, I checked. It was nowhere to be found. Was I down? Fuck yeah. Did I have a minute where I was like, *"another one bites the dust?"* Yep, but that was only for a minute. Why? Because the reviews came in. The readers loved the damn book. *Loved it.* Even better, *I* loved it. Better yet, I sold books. Lots of them. Not list lots, but lots for me.

Would it have been cool to make that list on that book? Fuck yeah. But it didn't happen and THAT'S OKAY!!! Did you read that last part? IT'S OKAY!!

I'm probably confusing the shit out of you, but bear with me. That's what we do in the Indie world is roll with it … so start rollin' with me.

When it comes to lists, you need to think beyond them. Yes, beyond them. I say this because, you can make a list once, and never make it again. Therefore, you need to plan out what your end goal is. All authors need to have a goal with putting out a book.

If your goal is to make a list, you need to move a lot of product. And let's be straight; for most of us to do that, we need to do that with a $0.99 release. (For those of you lucky enough to not have to do this, more power to ya. Personally, I can't; or, at least I haven't at this point.) Now, in doing this, you aren't going to make the money you could have made by choosing this step. If you sell eight thousand copies of your book at $0.99, you will make approximately $2800 on that book. If you had your price at $2.99 and sold eight thousand copies, you'd make $16,744. If your price is at $2.99 and you sold fifteen hundred copies, you'd make $3139. These are simple numbers so you can see the difference. Bottom line, at a higher price point, you have to sell less copies to make the money back you put in the book.

Would you make the list, YES! You'd hit your goal, but then you can't bitch and complain that you didn't make money with your latest release, because that was your choice. Your goal for that book was met. If you don't like the aftermath of that goal, then it's time you buckle up and rethink your goals.

It's okay to change your mind, too! We're all learning. WE'RE ALL LEARNING!

When I put out *Bound by Family*, my goal was to make money. The list would just be a nice perk IF IT HAPPNED. Therefore, my special preorder price was $2.99, and then I bumped that price up to $3.99 the day after release. Did I make money on that book? Fuck yeah. Did I make a list? Nope. But I achieved my goal! So, I call that release a success.

The lists are obtainable. If that's your goal, there are many ways to skew the sales in your favor. Such as putting out a release at $0 .99 and/or having a lengthy (three month) preorder, and then pimping and running the hell out of ads to make your book known. This has worked for many people and more power to them. That's their goal, and they made it!! Yay them!! Would this work for me? I don't know because I haven't tried it because it doesn't fit my goal.

Just know that whatever you decide your goal is, IT'S OKAY! You need to be you and decide what you want to do with your writing career. If you joined this world just to put out books and don't give a rat's ass if you sell any or make any lists, then more power to you. Most of us doing this, though, are looking to make sure we make money to support our families, put food on the table, and a roof over our heads. That is a personal choice that only you can make.

DO NOT ALLOW LISTS TO DEFINE YOU AS AN AUTHOR!! You never make a list, shit happens. It does not mean for one second that you aren't a great author. It doesn't mean that you suck and need to throw in the towel! NO, NO, NO! Making a list doesn't define you. It doesn't mean you're less than.

It doesn't mean that you can't make a LIVING at writing!

Yes, did you catch that last part? You can make a living at writing without making a list. I'm living proof of that. Am I telling you to quit your job and go to writing full-time? NO, NO, NO!!! That's for a whole different chapter of this series. What I'm saying is that you don't have to make the handy dandy lists in order to have a fulfilling job! Yes, JOB!

More to come, ladies and gents. Batten down the hatches!

Chelsea's Chat:

HELL IS A FOUR LETTER WORD.

List is a four letter word.

They are both bad.

gasp Oh no, she didn't ...

Yeah, I went there.

Look, let's get clear; lists make things bad. Not all lists, but in this case, the ones we are referring to are bad.

Well shit, CC, how can you say that? Umm ... simple. They bring out the worst in really good people.

Real deal. I am probably going to upset some people with how candid I get, but I went into this book wanting to be completely honest, raw, no holding back, honest in my words.

The first time I made *USA Today*, I cried.

Yes, I cried.

Not happy tears.

I had just signed a co-written project over to a publisher, which this is not a bad thing, people, so please do not read into my words. Within weeks of the trade, they put it on sale for $0.99. The book had only been out three months. I never do sales like this. I was worried about my brand.

(Pricing, sales, branding—we could do an entire other book on these. They are crucial, but I have to focus on lists right now).

The sale did well. The lists were announced, and *BOOM* ... it made it.

Except, my mind couldn't celebrate the moment. Nope, I jumped on a raft and let myself fly down the waterslide of my tears into the rabbit hole.

You see, I put my heart into every book I write. There are pieces of my life in all of them. And without my publisher, without a sale, I couldn't hack it. I wasn't good enough.

People close to me asked, *"CC, are you going to change all your covers now to say* USA Today Bestselling Author?" I replied, "No." And for a while, I didn't. Even to this day, it's not on all my covers.

I don't want to be defined because one week I managed to sell a shit ton. I want to be defined by my words, my work, my character, my integrity, and the impact I leave on others.

While everyone celebrated this milestone—and it was, I won't say it wasn't—I ached and felt less than.

Also, since this occurred on a traditionally published book that was co-written and on sale, you should know I walked away with less than $500 earned off those sales that week after all the cuts. So, if being traditionally published is an aspiration, please make sure you understand the income infrastructure.

Look, it's amazing to find your work on a list or to be up for some award. I would be full of shit if I said otherwise. But I want to be clear that it doesn't change your work, it doesn't change your talent.

I have been blessed to later make the *USA Today Bestsellers* list at full price on another title, but so far in my career, I have not achieved it without my publisher. Yes, you heard it right. I am not a bestseller on my self-published titles.

But, CC, you have been in the Amazon top 100 with the Hellions. Yeah, sure have. If the Zon was all that mattered, I guess I could use that bestseller word, but it's not. The lists that are equal in the industry are the three big lists we are referring to here.

Whether an author wants to say *International Bestselling Author* or *Erotica Bestselling Author* doesn't matter. If a book is good, it's good, period. Don't get hung up on what you can put before your name.

I promise it doesn't change your sales. Making a list once or twice doesn't promise to make it every release. Just look at my career.

It's easy to get sucked down in titles, but it doesn't have to be that way. Remember why you started writing. It's not sales, it's not money, and it damn sure ain't a title. It's the story that was in your head, begging to be told. Stick with that, be the person you are at your core, and the rest will one day follow or not, but I promise the not won't break you.

Lists Lists Lists Bullet Points

KNOW YOUR GOALS.

Stick to your goals.

Know the outcome of what you choose.

YOU DON'T NEED TO BE A *USA TODAY BESTSELLER*, *NYT* OR *WALL STREET JOURNAL* LIST HOLDER TO EARN A LIVING AT WRITING!

YOU ARE NOT A FAILURE BECAUSE YOU DIDN'T MAKE THE LIST!

In closing

Damn, I feel like we've only skimmed the surface with this book. And honestly, neither Chelsea or I even know if you want to read this stuff. This entire concept came on a whim. A text at 9 p.m. I sent CC the section on signings at 8 a.m. the next morning. Then, for the next couple of days, we went back and forth, adding different things. *Boom.*

Remember what we said at the beginning. This isn't a how-to book. It's just our experiences. Every author has different ones and some things work for one that don't work for another.

Let us know what you think about this. What would you like us to go deeper into? What things we didn't cover that we should?

Off the top of my head, building genuine relationships with other authors is one. A full-out budget for a book is another. If you would like a step by step something or other, I'm sure I can keep going, so I'm going to STOP!

But really, let us know.

This book actually turned into a therapy session that I guess we needed and didn't even know it. I know I, Ryan, feel good about it. Neither Chelsea or I have problems answering questions. At the same time, it becomes a lot at times when your FB PMs are out of control and your emails are sprouting devil horns. This book was a simple way for us to answer those questions that we get in a way that's us.

CC's addition here:

I hate social media and could write more on the how to deal with social media time suckers and making the shit work for you without losing your whole morning to it. If you have ever reached out to me on FB, Twitter (which I love and could so write a book all in hashtags. lol), Instagram, etc., and I didn't reply ... well, I hate social media. Nothing personal. I get overwhelmed easily, so sometimes—a lot of times—I turn the shit off. I can't handle it all. It's not you; it's me.

I also want to answer everyone and help everyone, but I can't do it and keep up my own schedule, so this book came from my desire to help yet not sure how to do it. Ryan sorted that for me, so here we are.

Now, if you email us, don't get all pissed off if we don't return the email right away! Both of us have a shit ton going on. CC and I have our collaborative book coming out in May, and we each have a biker book with our series we're writing. That's not saying that, if we get feedback, we won't be at our computers, typing back and forth like mad women. Because this is fun. And we all need a little fun in our lives, people.

Names said in this book were not intended to *name drop*, as some would call it. They are real experiences that were written to show you a perspective and hopefully get you to see something new. Photographers, cover designers, and formatters, or anyone else are mentioned from our own experiences. If you choose to check any of them out, we highly encourage you to check out their terms and conditions and contracts thoroughly. Things may have changed with them since our experiences, and we want you to have the most up-to-date factual information.

What we wrote is not stone or the Bible. It is full-out or experiences, and that goes for everyone/anyone mentioned in this book. If you're mentioned and you don't want to be for any reason, please email us. We're not here to piss you off. At least, not really.

We hope you've enjoyed our crazy and that you've gotten something out of this. Even if it's one thing, then it was worth your time, right? At least, I hope you see it that way. If you don't, then you don't.

No matter what, never give up on whatever your goals are. You can do this. We are proof of it.

Love Always,
   Ryan & Chelsea

And in closing …

What's next?

Indie Insider: Getting Started.

Consider this Marketing 101 for starting out. We have a feeling Marketing will take multiple books to cover at every stage in your career.

About Chelsea Camaron

USA Today bestselling author Chelsea Camaron is a small town Carolina girl with a big imagination. She's a wife and mom, chasing her dreams. She writes contemporary romance, erotic suspense, and psychological thrillers. She loves to write about blue-collar men who have real problems with a fictional twist. From mechanics to bikers to oil riggers to smokejumpers, bar owners, and beyond she loves a strong hero who works hard and plays harder.

Chelsea can be found at:
www.authorchelseacamaron.com

About Ryan Michele

Ryan Michele found her passion in bringing fictional characters to life. She loves being in an imaginative world where anything is possible, and she has a knack for special twists readers don't see coming.

She writes MC, Contemporary, Erotic, Paranormal, New Adult, Inspirational, and other romance-based genres. Whether it's bikers, wolf-shifters, mafia, etc., Ryan spends her time making sure her heroes are strong and her heroines match them at every turn. When she isn't writing, Ryan is a mom and wife living in rural Illinois and reading by her pond in the warm sun.

Come find Ryan:
www.authorryanmichele.net

INDIE INSIDER

BENIND THE PAGES

CHELSEA CAMARON
RYAN MICHELE

www.ingramcontent.com/pod-product-compliance
Lightning Source LLC
Chambersburg PA
CBHW071434180526
45170CB00001B/342